P9-DXH-123

03851649

OKANAGAN COLLEGE
LIBRARY
BRITISH COLUMBIA

K

The Impact of China and India on Sub-Saharan African Countries

Opportunities, Challenges and Policies

Oliver Morrissey
and Evious Zgovu

Commonwealth Secretariat

Commonwealth Secretariat
Marlborough House, Pall Mall
London SW1Y 5HX
United Kingdom

© Commonwealth Secretariat 2011

All rights reserved. No part of this publication may be reproduced, stored in a retrieval system, or transmitted in any form or by any means, electronic or mechanical, including photocopying, recording or otherwise without the permission of the publisher.

Published by the Commonwealth Secretariat

Edited by Tina Johnson
Designed by S.J.I. Services, New Delhi
Cover design by Tattersall Hammarling & Silk
Printed by CMP (uk) Ltd

Views and opinions expressed in this publication are the responsibility of the authors and should in no way be attributed to the institutions to which they are affiliated or to the Commonwealth Secretariat.

Wherever possible, the Commonwealth Secretariat uses paper sourced from sustainable forests or from sources that minimise a destructive impact on the environment.

Copies of this publication may be obtained from
Publications Section
Commonwealth Secretariat
Marlborough House
Pall Mall
London SW1Y 5HX
United Kingdom
Tel: +44 (0)20 7747 6534
Fax: +44 (0)20 7839 9081
Email: publications@commonwealth.int
Web: www.thecommonwealth.org/publications

A catalogue record for this publication is available from the British Library.

ISBN (paperback): 978-1-84929-055-5
ISBN (e-book): 978-1-84859-108-0

Contents

Tables and Figures

Appendix Tables

Abbreviations

ACP	African, Caribbean and Pacific countries
AGOA	African Growth Opportunity Act
CNPC	China National Petroleum Corporation
DAC	Development Assistance Committee (of the OECD)
EPA	Economic Partnership Agreement
EU	European Union
FDI	foreign direct investment
FOCAC	Forum on China–Africa Cooperation
GDP	gross domestic product
HS	Harmonized System
LDC	Least Developed Country
MFA	Multi-Fibre Agreement
OECD	Organisation for Economic Co-operation and Development
PPP	purchasing power parity
Sinopec	China Petroleum and Chemical Corporation
SSA	sub-Saharan Africa
UNCTAD	United Nations Conference on Trade and Development
WITS	World Integrated Trade Solution
WTO	World Trade Organization

Summary

China and India have become major trading partners for countries in sub-Saharan Africa (SSA) in the past decade and are becoming important sources of foreign investment (especially China). While SSA provides minerals and oil needed to meet rapidly growing demand for industrial inputs, benefiting exporters, China and India are also increasing their import penetration in the region, with some adverse effects on competing local labour-intensive industries in both domestic markets and third-country export markets. Thus increased trade with China and India represents opportunities and challenges, the balance of which varies across SSA countries. This report provides an assessment of the impacts and puts forward some recommendations.

Trade relations with China and India

Eight resource-rich SSA countries dominate exports to China and India and are the main beneficiaries. These are Angola, Congo, Equatorial Guinea, Nigeria and Sudan for crude oil; and Democratic Republic of the Congo, South Africa and Zambia for metals and ores. Other SSA countries export timber and soft commodities such as cash crops; fruits, nuts and vegetables; oils and resins; and seafood.

Imports are also concentrated; Nigeria and South Africa account for more than half of the value of Chinese and Indian imports into SSA. However, China and India have an increasing share of the import market in many SSA countries. For example, China accounts for over 10 per cent of imports in seven countries, and over 20 per cent in Ethiopia and Madagascar. India has a larger import share than China in a number of SSA countries, mostly those located on or close to the Indian Ocean.

The largest import shares for China and India are industrial goods such as machinery and equipment, vehicles, iron and steel and, for India in particular, pharmaceutical products and cereals. In these products they are likely to be displacing suppliers from the rest of the world. China is more likely than India at present to provide imports that compete with SSA local producers, such as furniture, footwear and ceramic products.

The basic message in terms of a development-oriented long-term SSA export strategy is to concentrate on value addition (processing) to their resources. SSA countries should not overlook opportunities to develop garment exports, but these may not be a secure platform for long-term export growth. There is little evidence that China and India can assist the integration of SSA into global value chains, although they are often important investors in the garment sector. In some countries China and India have significant shares of textiles imports for this sector, but they are likely to have invested to avail of trade preferences. This suggests that the SSA countries are positioned in a fragmented production structure rather than supported in developing an independent position in the global supply chain.

Trade agreements, especially Economic Partnership Agreements (EPAs) with the European Union (EU), may threaten the shares of China and India in SSA imports, eliciting a response. The potential of tariffs as a policy instrument for protection and revenue will diminish. In the future, SSA trade policy should focus on exports. Domestic producers, including those competing with imports, should be the focus of agriculture and industry policy.

Investment from China and India

An important observation is that in practice it is difficult to clearly distinguish between foreign direct investment (FDI) and aid; for China in particular, many activities combine elements of both. Clearly, Chinese FDI in SSA is quite concentrated, with Nigeria, South Africa, Sudan and Zambia having the largest stock while Angola and Equatorial Guinea are more recent hosts. In general, China is investing in the same mineral-rich SSA countries that attract global FDI in general. Indian FDI is at much lower levels and concentrated traditionally in Mauritius and more recently in countries such as Côte d'Ivoire, Senegal and Sudan.

Chinese aid to SSA, amounting to about US$1 billion per annum and mostly in the form of concessional loans (or debt relief), is concentrated in the mineral resource-exporting countries and mainly directed to infrastructure. It is often tied to Chinese firms and linked to trade with China. Indian aid is focused on infrastructure projects in Nigeria and Sudan and lines of credit to West African countries. Indian aid levels are currently quite low (less than US$20 million per annum) but projected to rise significantly.

Chinese aid and investment has delivered benefits to SSA countries, but there are many reasons to believe that the dynamic benefits are less than they could be. Specifically, Chinese aid (and investment) appears to have few linkages with the local economy.

In terms of investment, SSA governments should be aware that FDI can be transient in nature. This is most likely if the investment is motivated by accessing trade preferences that may themselves be temporary. Investment motivated by securing access to resources is more long term, but SSA must ensure it receives the right price. In this regard, a number of policy recommendations are summarised in general terms:

- Resource-exporting countries should ensure that they receive a competitive market price and that the revenue from exports is invested in promoting development.
- Producers of soft commodities should be supported in identifying opportunities in China and Indian export markets through the provision of market information and access to networks.
- Effective export diversification should be based on identifying value-adding activities to process available resources.
- Imports from China and India can compete with some domestic producers, but governments should only support promising local firms with the potential to be more competitive.

- SSA governments should ensure that aid and investment projects by China and India contribute to the local economy and development by putting greater focus on sectors and projects with strong linkages with the rest of the economy.
- Investment by China and India is motivated by their own commercial interests and cannot be assumed to assist the integration of SSA producers into global value chains. The experience with garments cautions that such investment can be transitory.
- More effective engagement with China and India is possible if SSA countries co-operate to increase their bargaining power and encouragement regional investment projects.
- Relations with China and India will be affected by trade agreements with other parties, notably EPAs with the EU. Whilst EPAs may allow the EU to capture some market share from China and India in SSA imports, as they enhance preferential access to the EU, they will also make SSA more attractive for investment.

1

Introduction

The last decade has seen the rise of a number of developing countries, leading to a 'shift in global wealth' (OECD, 2010) and a rebalancing of economic powers. China and India have been the most prominent and have attracted the most attention, but others such as Brazil and Russia are close behind. This shift has been most evident in global patterns of trade. 'Between 1990 and 2008 world trade expanded almost four-fold, but South–South trade multiplied more than ten times and developing countries now account for around 37% of global trade' (OECD, 2010: 18). Economic (and political) relationships between developing countries (South–South) are more important now than they have ever been; developing countries trade more with each other, and more capital (investment and aid) flows between them absolutely and relative to their relationship with developed countries. This changing economic landscape will be an important influence on their future performance.

Although countries in Africa, and especially sub-Saharan Africa (SSA), still account for a small proportion of world trade, they have benefited from the growth of large developing countries through increased demand for their exports of primary commodities and associated investment flows. Recent data bear this out: 'the share of non-African developing countries in Africa's total merchandise trade increased from 8 per cent in 1980 to 29 per cent in 2008 and their share in inward foreign direct investment (FDI) flows to the region rose from an average of 12 per cent over the period 1995–1999 to 16 per cent over the period 2000–2008' (UNCTAD, 2010: 1). Against this backdrop two countries are the most important for Africa: China and India. There is a large body of literature that shows that the growth of China and India has affected SSA through various linkages including trade, FDI, aid and debt relief, and migration of Chinese and Indian workers.[1]

Although China has had economic relationships with many SSA countries since the 1960s, it is only in the last decade or so that it has become a major economic partner. This is most obvious in respect of primary commodity exports, where China has become the most buoyant market, but also relates to imports of manufactures, foreign investment and aid. 'The value of trade between Africa and China increased nearly tenfold between 2000 and 2008 ... making China Africa's second largest trade partner after the United States, and its largest developing country partner by far' (UNCTAD, 2010: 30). While not of the same magnitude, there have also been relations with India, often reflecting links with Asian business families in East Africa. As the Indian economy is now growing almost as fast as China's, it is also becoming a major trading partner with SSA. An assessment of the opportunities and challenges associated with expanding economic relations with China and India is thus essential to identify appropriate planning and policy responses for SSA countries.

As the development of China and India progresses, SSA countries are in a prime situation as sources of raw materials. For these expanding economies, SSA can provide the mainly cheap minerals and oil needed to meet rapidly growing demand for industrial inputs.[2] In turn, China and India are low-cost exporters of manufactures with increasing import penetration in SSA. While this will increase the welfare of consumers (through cheaper imports), it may undermine competing local labour-intensive industries (such as clothing) in domestic markets and also in third-country export markets. Thus increased trade with China and India represents both opportunities and challenges.

That China and India are having an impact on SSA is not disputed; what is not clear is the precise nature of the impact and how it varies across countries. Existing analysis has often been at high levels of aggregation (at least in terms of imports). This gives a partial picture of the effects, especially how they differ depending on the country context. The aims of this report are to provide a better understanding of the impact of China and India on SSA by focusing not only on countries but also on the sectors/products affected. More generally, it is intended to provide a clear understanding of the impact of interactions related to production, trade, investment and aid flows, with a view to inform policy measures to maximise opportunities and address the threats and challenges.

Context and issues

In the past 10 years China has become SSA's third most important trading partner (if the EU is treated as one unit); the value of Sino–African trade increased from about US$5 billion in 1997 to US$74 billion in 2007 (Taylor, 2010: 1). China is now the major source of demand for primary exports from SSA countries. China and India together have a massive population of 2.5 billion inhabitants, representing 37 per cent of the total world population (China 20 per cent and India 17 per cent in 2008). Over the past decade their economies have experienced rapid transformation and development. Between 2002 and 2008 China's gross domestic product (GDP) per capita in purchasing power parity (PPP) terms increased from US$4,600 to US$5,300, while India's GDP per capita rose from US$2,540 to US$2,700, and their combined GDP accounted for an estimated 15 per cent of world GDP in 2008. Recent World Trade Organization (WTO, 2009) data show that in 2008 China was the third largest trading nation after the United States and Germany (with exports representing 9 per cent of world exports and imports representing 7 per cent of world imports); by mid-2010 it had overtaken Germany. Given their size and tremendous growth (averaging 10 per cent annually in China and 6 per cent in India over the past decade), they have become major global economies (the implications of which are a focus of OECD, 2010).

The steady economic growth of both countries is partly due to trade liberalisation, a rapidly growing supply of low-cost skilled and semi-skilled labour, and FDI attracted by the growing market sizes and favourable investment and low production cost conditions. As a result China's exports have increased relative to imports, leading to large trade surpluses with almost all other leading global economies and developing countries. Between 1996 and 2008 China's exports increased nine-fold from US$151 billion to US$1,428 billion, while its imports increased eight-fold from US$139 billion to US$1,133 billion. Imports largely comprise raw materials, oil, metals and precious minerals needed to meet growing domestic demand and production for export.[3]

China became a member of the WTO on 11 December 2001, while India is an original member of the organisation (constituted on 1 January 1995). Both countries have stepped up their involvement in regional and bilateral trade and investment agreements, and also offer some developing and least developed countries (LDCs) preferential access to their domestic markets as well as debt relief and aid. As a result, they are now exerting substantial economic 'pull and push gravitational forces' in an increasingly globalised and integrated world economy. These forces offer fundamental opportunities and pose challenges with both direct and indirect, complementary and competitive impacts from the perspective of other economies, and have generated interest among policy-makers and researchers in developed and developing countries alike.

China's appetite for imports has been growing rapidly over the past decade as its economy has expanded. It needs raw materials and other inputs to sustain its growth. The strategic importance of Africa, a traditionally rich source of raw materials, was reflected in the Forum on China–Africa Cooperation (FOCAC) that first met in Beijing in 2000 (and subsequently met in Addis Ababa in 2003, Beijing in 2006 and Cairo in 2009). FOCAC established a new era of trade co-operation between China and Africa, especially SSA. Since then Africa has become more important as a source of oil and of raw materials needed by the Chinese manufacturing sector. Similar relations are being established with India, which declared commitments on aid, market access and investment at the India–Africa Forum Summit in 2008.

Under the FOCAC, China grants non-reciprocal duty-free access to 190 products imported from 28 African LDCs. Chinese firms have also heavily increased investments in Africa, particularly in the oil sector (in Angola, Nigeria and Sudan), infrastructure construction projects (e.g., the US$8 billion Lagos–Kano railway project and a US$300 million highway upgrading in Nigeria), textiles and clothing (in part to circumvent US and European limits on Chinese textile and clothing exports) and mining (e.g., a US$200 million copper project in Zambia). Under the India-Africa Forum, India has offered tariff-free access for most exports of LDCs (33 in SSA).

China and India will continue to be a major source of demand for SSA exports, offering significant trade opportunities to countries with mineral resources. On the other hand, imports represent a challenge to domestic manufacturing sectors in SSA countries. Although the major products involved are machinery and equipment, vehicles and pharmaceutical products that do not compete with local industries (except perhaps in South Africa), Chinese consumer goods (electronics, clothing and shoes) have captured an increasing market share in SSA imports (and Indian imports include processed foods). The nature of this trade-off affects SSA countries differently as in general the countries that export the most to China and India are not the same as the ones for which penetration by Chinese and Indian imports is greatest.

Aims of the report

The primary aim of this report is to quantify the importance of China and India as economic partners with SSA countries. The main focus is on trade flows for which reasonably comprehensive data are available, exploring import and export patterns and identifying the main SSA countries and sectors involved. A secondary focus is on investment and aid flows from China and India to SSA, although data here are more limited (especially for India).

Based on a review of data and literature on the levels and impacts of trade, investment and aid flows between SSA and China and India, the report's objective is to inform policy responses and strategies for enhancing the ability of SSA countries to exploit the opportunities and enable them to integrate their economies into more lucrative global value chains. It analyses sectors/products benefiting from SSA's increased engagement with India and China; assesses the implications of this increased engagement for SSA regional integration and preferential trade arrangements with developed countries; identifies SSA countries benefiting from increased engagement; and addresses related concerns and challenges.

Outline of the report

Whereas data are available to demonstrate the importance of China and India as trading partners, observations regarding investment and aid (mostly related to China) are often based on anecdotal evidence as hard data are difficult to compile. This is reflected in the structure of the report, as a more detailed analysis of trade relations is possible than of the other areas.

Section 2 documents the importance of China and India as trading partners. Although the importance of India lags behind China, both are major sources of demand for raw material (natural resource) exports from a similar set of SSA countries (though fewer in the case of India); they thus provide an opportunity for SSA resource-rich exporters. Both are also increasing their share of SSA imports, especially in textiles and clothing, machinery and light manufactures (in particular consumer goods). This tends to affect different SSA countries, especially those with competing local producers facing the challenge of adjusting to increased import competition.

Section 3 focuses on investment and aid flows to SSA from China, with limited information for India. Although still a relatively small source of capital inflows compared to developed countries, China is increasingly becoming a major player on the continent, especially in a select number of countries. It is worth noting that distinguishing between FDI and aid poses a practical challenge as, for China in particular, many activities combine elements of both. As neither China nor India adhere to the Organisation for Economic Co-operation and Development-Development Assistance Committee (OECD-DAC) definition of aid, it is particularly difficult to quantify such flows; recognising this, UNCTAD (2010) refers to 'official flows' to encompass aid.

Section 4 identifies opportunities and challenges faced in different SSA countries with a view to deriving policy recommendations. The discussion reflects the broader context of economic relations between SSA and developed countries and any relevance for increasing

diversification of SSA export opportunities. A particular focus is on the implications for SSA countries in developing coherent investment strategies.

Notes

1. See for example, Ajakaiye (2006), Bosshard (2008), Finger (2008), Giovannetti and Sanfilippo (2009), Gu (2009), Kaplinsky (2007), Kaplinsky and Morris (2008; 2009), Minson (2008) and Oyejide *et al.* (2009).

2. Countries in Latin America and the Middle East are important sources of raw materials and oil for China and India as well; some are also significant trading partners with Africa (notably Brazil, Turkey and the United Arab Emirates). The West is an important source of intermediate inputs, metals (e.g., steel) and FDI.

3. India's exports rose five-fold from US$33 billion in 1996 to US$182 billion in 2008 while imports rose eight-fold from US$39 billion to US$316 billion over the same period (World Bank via WITS database).

2

Review of Trade Relationships

Trade is the principal sphere of economic activity through which the recent growth of China and India has affected the global balance of economic strength (see OECD, 2010). Because of low unit labour costs, modern production technologies founded on long and intensive investment in research and development, developed logistical infrastructure and aggressive export marketing practices, both countries are serious competitive global exporters of various light manufactures and high-end products. This is most pronounced for China, which has been one of the three largest exporting economies since about 2007. This contrasts with 1993 when China's merchandise exports were barely a fifth of the US share of global exports (at 12.6 per cent, then the world's largest merchandise goods exporter). The expansion of China's merchandise exports has squeezed the relative importance of other industrialised economies including France, Japan and the United Kingdom (see Appendix Tables A9 and A10). India's gain in share has been modest relative to China's but is on the increase.

Over the period 2000–2008 and especially recently, China and India recorded more robust growth in trade than the United States, Japan and EU (27) countries as a group (Tables A9 and A10). In volume terms, although world exports only increased by 5 per cent per annum on average over 2000–2008, Chinese exports grew by 20.5 per cent and Indian exports by 12 per cent (WTO, 2009: Table I.2). In value terms Chinese export performance was even more impressive, with growth of 24 per cent per annum over 2000–2008, twice the rate of world export growth (Table A10). Africa's trade grew by an average rate of 18 per cent per annum over the same period, largely driven by China's demand for commodities from the continent. China and India exhibited remarkable resilience by sustaining trade growth even during the global economic downturn after 2007. In 2008 African exports grew by 28 per cent in value terms, reflecting robust demand from China in particular (Table A10).

The global growth of emerging economies has affected the geographical pattern of African trade: 'the share of non-African developing countries in Africa's extra-regional trade increased from 19.6 per cent in 1995 to 32.5 per cent in 2008, while their share of the region's total trade rose from 15.4 per cent to 28.7 per cent over the same period' (UNCTAD, 2010: 30). China is now Africa's major trading partner after the EU and the USA, 'and its largest developing country partner by far. China alone now accounts for about 11 per cent of Africa's external trade and is the region's largest source of imports' (UNCTAD, 2010: 30).

While the growth of China and India has been phenomenal, potential impacts on SSA should be seen in context. First, SSA countries are largely producers and exporters of primary commodities (the first, and weakest, point in the global value chain). Empirical trade literature shows that primary commodities tend to face a secular decline in their terms of trade owing to differential rises in prices of manufactures at higher stages of the chain. Prior to the 2000s, SSA countries tended to face falling relative prices of their exports. The recent increases in commodity prices driven by demand from China and India have been a clear benefit to SSA exporters of these commodities. As discussed below, however, this has not been a benefit to all SSA countries.

Second, SSA maintains strong traditional trade ties with the developed countries premised on historical (mainly with Europe) and preferential terms of access through trade preference schemes (especially for the EU and USA). Developed countries absorbed over 60 per cent of Africa's exports, estimated at US$558 billion in 2008 alone, while Asia as a whole absorbed 20 per cent.

Third, not all SSA countries, sectors and products have been affected in the same way. It is well documented that the SSA countries that have benefited most from China's growth are those endowed with and exporting raw materials and commodities in the extractive industries. Five countries accounted for 84 per cent of African exports to China in 2008 (UNCTAD, 2010: 34): Angola (48 per cent), Sudan (15 per cent), South Africa (9 per cent), Congo (7 per cent) and Equatorial Guinea (5 per cent). Interestingly, five countries also accounted for 84 per cent of exports to India: Nigeria (47 per cent), South Africa (14 per cent), Egypt (10 per cent), Angola (8 per cent) and Morocco (5 per cent). The greater importance of Nigeria and North African countries for India is also true for other emerging countries such as Brazil, Korea and Turkey (ibid.: 34). As discussed below, a larger set of SSA countries have benefited from aid, debt relief and infrastructure projects with a less direct trade connection (though some of this potentially also benefits the countries' productive capacity).

While some exporting countries benefit, all SSA domestic markets are experiencing an influx of relatively low-priced Chinese and Indian manufactures, and SSA exporters are also grappling with competition in regional and third-country export markets where they have traditionally sold their narrow range of industrial exports (especially clothing). Notwithstanding these caveats, the general global increase in commodity prices and capital inflows into SSA driven by growth in China and India represent an important impetus for SSA development. The challenge for SSA, so riddled with productive and logistical capacity constraints, is how best to manage both the opportunities and challenges to maximise the development impact.

The rise of Sino–African trade has received considerable attention (van Dijk, 2009). Exports to China from SSA were worth about US$20 billion in 2005, whereas Chinese imports were worth over US$7 billion. Mineral fuels (oil) accounted for some 70 per cent of exports and other minerals about 16 per cent. Manufactures only accounted for 10 per cent, with South Africa the only country with significant exports in this category. Typically one primary commodity dominates the trade; for example, since 2005 Nigeria has become an important exporter of oil to China, which also accounts for almost two-thirds of Sudan's oil production.

The economic relationship between China and Africa has been strengthened through the Forum on China–Africa Cooperation (FOCAC) that has met four times since 2000.

At the 2009 FOCAC Conference in Cairo, China made a number of commitments to further co-operation regarding trade, investment and aid or debt relief (UNCTAD, 2010: 15). It offered to provide US$10 billion in concessional loans and to support co-operation in science and technology, agriculture, health, education and energy projects to mitigate the effects of climate change. China also proposed to phase in tariff-free access for most products from African LDCs that had diplomatic relations.

Trade between India and Africa 'increased from US$7.3 billion in 2000 to US$31 billion in 2008' (UNCTAD, 2010: 17) and this encouraged a strengthening of relationships. India convened the First India–Africa Forum Summit in New Delhi from 8–9 April 2008 and made a number of commitments (Katti *et al.*, 2009: 4). Aid to Africa was to be increased, with almost US$2 billion in lines of credit (mostly for agriculture and food production, infrastructure and energy sectors) and US$500 million in grants for human resources and capacity building. India also announced a Duty Free Tariff Preference Scheme for LDCs covering most products. This provides opportunities for SSA countries to increase exports of products such as cotton, cocoa, aluminium ores, copper ores, cashew nuts, cane sugar, ready-made garments and fish.

Importance of China and India for SSA exports

Demand from China, and in particular the way this has been sustained despite the 2007–2008 global crisis, is the principal determinant of the increase in SSA export earnings since the early 2000s. Strong growth in demand by China for metals and minerals – particularly

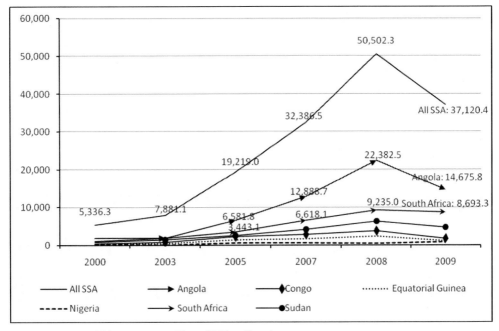

Figure 2.1. Major SSA exporters to China (US$ millions)
Source: Authors analysis using data from WITS.

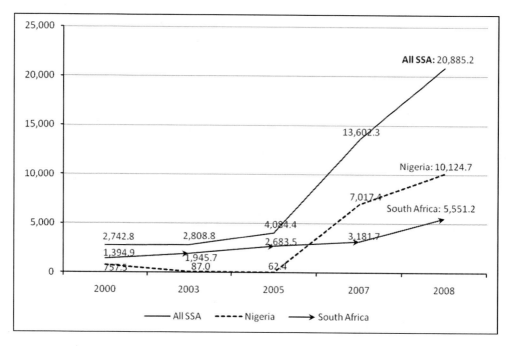

Figure 2.2. Major SSA exporters to India (US$ millions)
Source: Authors analysis using data from WITS.

copper, iron ore and nickel – and for some commodities by India has fuelled the rise in mineral commodity prices since 2002; China's imports increased most over 1990–2003 in the fuels, minerals and metals categories (Mayer and Fajarnes, 2008: 86). The SSA share in China's primary commodities imports grew rapidly over 1999–2003 for all major categories, except ores and metals, and especially for crude petroleum (ibid.: 87).

This is illustrated in Figure 2.1, which shows the rapid growth of SSA exports to China over 2000–2009; by 2008 the value of exports was about 10 times the 2000 level, and even after a decline in 2009 (largely accounted for by a decline in oil imports from Angola) it was still about seven times the 2000 level. Angola has been the major beneficiary (mostly oil), but South Africa has also been a significant beneficiary with a more diversified range of products (nickel, copper, iron and other ores, as well as some manufactures). Figure 2.2 shows that the magnitude of growth in exports to India has been similar, albeit at less than half the level and concentrated in Nigeria (oil) and South Africa (ores and some manufactures). This concentration in a few countries is typical of SSA exports more generally:

> In 2008, the five largest African exporters to developing countries accounted for 67.5 per cent of the regions' total exports while the top 10 accounted for 89.2 per cent ... Africa's exports to developed countries are similarly concentrated with the top five and top 10 exporters accounting for 69.2 and 86.5 per cent of total exports respectively in 2008. The largest exporters to developing countries and to developed countries are largely the same even though there are some shifts in their rank and importance. Perhaps the most striking

Table 2.1. Major SSA exporters to China (% SSA exports to China), 2000–2009

	2000	2003	2005	2008	2009
Angola	34.53	27.99	34.25	44.32	39.54
Congo	6.07	10.34	11.85	7.39	4.68
Dem. Rep. of Congo	0.02	0.33	0.91	3.14	3.06
Equatorial Guinea	5.99	5.23	7.48	4.49	2.84
Nigeria	5.75	0.91	2.74	1.01	2.42
South Africa	19.44	23.35	17.91	18.29	23.42
Sudan	13.71	18.29	13.60	12.53	12.62
Zambia	1.30	0.61	1.31	1.03	3.43
Total (top 8)	86.81	87.05	90.07	92.19	92.01

Source: Authors analysis using data from WITS.

Table 2.2. Major SSA exporters to India (% SSA exports to India), 2000–2008

	2000	2003	2005	2007	2008
Angola	0.00	0.00	0.07	6.77	6.17
Congo	0.32	0.15	1.00	0.62	2.39
Dem. Rep. of Congo	0.01	0.00	0.13	0.13	0.55
Equatorial Guinea	0.00	0.01	0.00	0.53	0.40
Nigeria	27.61	3.10	1.53	51.59	48.48
South Africa	50.85	69.27	65.71	23.39	26.58
Sudan	0.27	1.08	0.68	1.78	2.61
Zambia	0.49	0.68	0.85	0.53	0.67
Total (top 8)	79.56	74.29	69.96	85.34	87.85

Source: Authors analysis using data from WITS.

of these is Angola. While Angola accounted for 9.5 per cent of Africa's exports to developed countries in 2008, making it the fifth largest African exporter, it was by far Africa's largest exporter to developing countries, accounting for 26.1 per cent. (UNCTAD, 2010: 32)

Tables 2.1 and 2.2 report the shares of the largest eight exporters in total SSA exports to China (2000–2009) and India (2000–2008) respectively. Perhaps the most interesting point is that the same eight countries (and, by implication, commodities) dominate exports to both countries (even if the ranking varies and export growth to India lags behind that to China by a number of years). These eight exporters accounted for 87 per cent of SSA exports to China in 2000 rising to 92 per cent in 2009; Angola's share varied between 28 and 44 per cent, South Africa between 18 and 33 per cent with Sudan consistently around 13 per cent. The eight countries increased their share of SSA exports to India from 70–80 per cent in the early 2000s to almost 90 per cent by 2008; Nigeria (with about half since 2007) and South Africa (over half until 2005 and about a quarter since then) dominate. Angola, Congo, Equatorial Guinea, Nigeria and Sudan are all major exporters of crude oil to China and India; Democratic Republic of the Congo, South Africa and Zambia benefit from exports of metals and ores.

This concentration of exports in particular countries is also reflected in, as it is largely due to, a concentration in particular (primary) commodities:

> While primary products accounted for 55 per cent of African exports to non-African developing countries in 1995, their share rose to 75 per cent in 2008. Over the same period, the share of resource-based manufactures in African exports to non-African developing countries fell from 27 to 15 per cent and that of low, medium and high technology manufactures from 18 to 10 per cent. (UNCTAD, 2010: 36)

Table 2.3. Chinese imports at HS2 level (if SSA > 5%), 2008

HS2	Value (US$ '000)	RSA %	Other SSA %	All SSA %	Rest of world %
All	1,132,562,161	0.8	3.6	4.5	95.5
09	101,158	0.6	4.7	5.3	94.7
18	312,958	0.0	36.2	36.2	63.8
24	787,784	0.4	19.0	19.4	80.6
26	85,936,803	4.7	2.9	7.6	92.4
27	169,251,777	0.1	21.0	21.0	79.0
44	8,023,379	0.0	12.3	12.3	87.7
71	7,547,713	22.6	0.9	23.5	76.5
81	1,317,057	0.9	29.1	29.9	70.1
99	4,407,629	35.2	0.0	35.2	64.8

Note: Percentage shares are rounded, hence sums of RSA% and Other SSA% may not equal to 'All SSA'.
Source: Derived from Appendix Table A6.

Table 2.4. Indian imports at HS2 level (if SSA > 5%), 2008

HS2	Value (US$ '000)	RSA %	Other SSA %	All SSA %	Rest of world %
Total	315,712,106	1.8	4.9	6.6	93.4
07	1,464,725	0.0	5.6	5.6	94.4
08	1,171,244	0.2	49.0	49.2	50.8
09	277,494	0.0	14.8	14.8	85.2
12	155,144	0.6	28.4	29.0	71.0
13	84,989	0.0	12.0	12.0	88.0
18	58,264	0.1	35.7	35.8	64.2
24	17,296	0.0	17.4	17.4	82.6
26	5,250,223	6.3	8.3	14.5	85.5
27	115,880,438	0.8	11.1	11.9	88.1
28	4,881,061	13.6	4.1	17.7	82.3
41	484,938	0.1	4.9	5.1	94.9
44	1,478,846	0.0	17.7	17.7	82.3
47	865,661	5.1	0.1	5.3	94.7
51	320,601	6.1	0.5	6.6	93.4
52	710,955	0.1	16.7	16.9	83.1
71	35,093,294	8.1	0.2	8.3	91.7
76	1,590,317	9.3	1.8	11.2	88.8
78	445,564	0.6	6.8	7.4	92.6
93	15,821	41.0	0.1	41.1	58.9

Note: Percentage shares are rounded, hence sums of RSA% and Other SSA% may not equal to 'All SSA'.
Source: Derived from Appendix Table A7.

Tables 2.3 and 2.4 report the major commodities (at the HS2[1] level) imported from SSA by China and India respectively (as shares of imports). In value terms, for both countries, the major commodities exported by SSA are mineral fuels (HS27), ores (HS26) and precious stones and metals (HS71, 76, 78 and 81). In the early 2000s Africa accounted for about a quarter of China's imports of crude oil, but this was a rapidly growing market for African exporters: 'between 2003 and 2004, China's petroleum imports increased by more than 40 per cent, accounting for more than 30 per cent of the incremental global oil demand' (Mayer and Fajarnes, 2008: 88). Although the export values are relatively small, SSA countries have high shares in Chinese and Indian imports of various agricultural cash crops such as coffee (HS09), cocoa (HS18), tobacco (HS24), fruits, nuts and vegetables (HS07–08) and oils and resins (HS12–13), the latter two being more important for India. In fact, although the value of exports is greater for China, it is more diversified for India. In addition to the agricultural commodities, SSA also has a good share in Indian imports of chemicals (HS28, mostly from South Africa – from which India also imports arms, HS93), hides (HS41), wood pulp

(HS47) and wool (HS51). Subsequent growth in demand from India thus offers potential benefits to a wide range of SSA exporters (it should be noted that China also imports many of these products, and although the SSA share is lower the export value may be similar).

Given the importance of its domestic construction sector and the rapid growth of furniture exports, China imports significant amounts of wood (HS44) from SSA, as does India. As of 2003, 'China sources over 20 per cent of its log imports from Africa, while China is the destination of about 13 per cent of Africa's log exports' (Mayer and Fajarnes, 2008: 92). In the early 2000s, timber exports were mainly from Congo, Equatorial Guinea and Gabon. Although there are many concerns about the practices of logging companies and the need for sustainable management of timber resources, this will remain an important export sector.

India and China are also important markets for cotton (HS52); SSA accounts for almost 17 per cent of Indian cotton imports, and although the share for China is low, this is relative to a much larger market. As China is the world's leading consumer of cotton, it not only provides demand (in 2003 China accounted for a fifth of African cotton exports) but also exerts upward pressure on world prices (Mayer and Fajarnes, 2008: 92). The SSA producers that supply China with cotton – mainly Benin, Burkina Faso and Mali – have benefited significantly in export earnings. There is also potential for SSA producers to increase exports of fish and shellfish to China and India, and there may be potential in respect of other foods. Thus, although to date the significant export benefits have been limited to about 10 countries providing minerals and crude oil, there are future opportunities for other SSA countries to expand exports of soft commodities (discussed further below).

Implications for SSA imports

Although SSA exporters benefit from their growth, China and India provide intense import competition in SSA markets (see Appendix Tables A3–A5 on the importance of China and India in terms of SSA imports for 2003, 2005 and 2008). Between 2003 and 2008 total SSA imports (for the sample with available data) grew from US$70.5 billion to US$189.5 billion. South Africa and Nigeria accounted for the bulk of SSA imports; the share of South Africa rose from 36 per cent in 2003 to 40 per cent in 2008 while Nigeria's share fell from 16 per cent to 13 per cent. Other important SSA countries in terms of import levels are Ethiopia, Ghana, Kenya, Madagascar, Mauritius, Sudan and Uganda. Imports from other SSA countries (intra-SSA trade) appeared to fall between 2003 and 2008 (this may reflect the fact that 2008 data covers many fewer countries), although the growth in the shares of China and India is mostly at the expense of the rest of the world.

The rise in imports from China and India over time has been sustained. The share of imports from China (India) rose continuously from 5.7 per cent (1.3 per cent) in 2003 to 10.7 per cent (4.2 per cent) in 2008 while imports from within SSA fell from 17.5 per cent in 2003 to 14.1 per cent in 2008. The combined shares of China and India surpassed the intra-SSA share in 2008. Certain individual SSA countries (Ethiopia, Madagascar, Nigeria, South Africa and Sudan) consistently imported more from China alone than they imported from the whole of SSA. The bulk of such imports are mostly machinery and mechanical appliances (HS84 and 85), which most SSA countries do not have the capacity to produce.

Table 2.5. SSA Countries with China or India import share > 5%

Country	China share (%)			India share (%)		
	2003	2005	2008	2003	2005	2008
Benin	7.1	8.8		1.7	1.6	
Burundi	0.9	4.2	7.3	0.0	4.1	5.0
Cameroon	4.0	5.2		1.5	1.3	
Côte d'Ivoire	3.5	3.1	6.9	0.0	1.4	1.7
Ethiopia	11.7	12.6	20.2	0.0	6.0	7.3
The Gambia	5.1	9.3	10.8	0.0	4.7	1.7
Ghana	5.6	8.1	11.7	0.0	3.4	4.3
Kenya	2.5	5.2	8.4	0.0	5.6	11.8
Madagascar	14.8	13.9	21.0	4.0	5.9	4.7
Mauritius	8.4	9.8	11.5	0.0	6.9	23.9
Niger	9.4	5.5	12.6	3.2	3.9	2.3
Rwanda	1.9	3.0	8.4	0.0	3.6	3.5
South Africa	6.4	9.0	11.3	1.2	2.0	2.6
Sudan	10.7	17.9	7.9	5.0	4.3	3.5
Togo	4.1	13.2		1.4	2.4	
Uganda	5.1	5.3	8.1	7.4	6.4	10.4
United Rep. of Tanzania	5.4	6.9		7.8	5.9	

Source: Appendix Tables A3–A5.

Table 2.5 lists the SSA countries for which China and/or India accounted for more than 5 per cent of imports by the mid to late 2000s. The steady increase in import penetration by both countries since 2003 is evident (although the data can be very variable from year to year – imports from India appear under-reported in 2003 while sudden peaks may reflect unusual activity in a particular year). By 2008 (where the data are rather incomplete), China accounted for over 10 per cent of imports for seven countries and over 20 per cent for Ethiopia and Madagascar. Although SSA, overall and for individual countries that export minerals, tends to have a trade surplus with China, there is nevertheless concern about the effect of Chinese imports on domestic producers in certain sectors, especially textiles and garments and consumer electrical and electronic goods (Taylor, 2010: 65). Madagascar is an example where China appears to supply the textiles for the growing garment (export) sector.

Although lagging behind China, India's import penetration is growing rapidly. It had a larger import share than China in a number of SSA countries mostly on or close to the Indian Ocean, such as Comoros, Kenya, Malawi, Mauritius, Mozambique, Seychelles, Uganda and United Republic of Tanzania. Most of these have traditionally had a significant expatriate Indian business community so that informal networks are well established; the Indo–African Chamber of Commerce and Industry has been established since 1985 and provides market information covering India and most African countries.

Table 2.6. Main SSA imports from China and India at HS2 level

HS2	Description	China	India
		N	N
02	Meat and edible meat offal		1
07	Edible vegetables, certain roots and tubers		1
10	Cereals	1	10
15	Animal or vegetable fats & oils	1	
25	Salt, sulphur, earth & stone, plaster	1	
27	Mineral fuels, oils		7
28	Inorganic chemicals		1
30	Pharmaceutical products		22
31	Fertilisers	1	
34	Soap; waxes; polish; candles	1	
39	Plastics and articles thereof		1
40	Rubber and articles thereof	1	1
44	Wood and articles of wood; charcoal	1	
51	Wool & animal hair, yarn & woven fabric	1	
52	Cotton, yarn and woven fabric	2	2
62	Apparel, not knitted or crocheted	1	
64	Footwear	3	
69	Ceramic products	2	
71	Pearls, precious stones	1	
72	Iron and steel	6	9
73	Articles of iron or steel	11	2
76	Aluminium and articles thereof		2
82	Tools, implements, cutlery, of base metal	1	
84	Machinery & mechanical	22	13
85	Electric machinery; electronic equipment	23	11
87	Vehicles (not railway); parts	12	15
94	Furniture and furnishings	4	

Note: N reports the number of countries for which the relevant HS2 product is in the 'top four' imports from China or India for the 24 SSA countries in Appendix Table A8.

Although import shares have increased dramatically, this does not necessarily imply increased competition with local producers; in many sectors China and India are likely to be displacing imports from the rest of the world. Table 2.6 lists the major products (by import share at the HS2 level) imported from China and India according to the number of SSA countries for which they rank in the 'top four' imports (Table A8 provides the details for 24 SSA countries). The major products imported from China are electrical machinery and equipment (HS85, in the top four for 23 countries), mechanical machinery (HS84, 22 countries), vehicles (HS87, 12 countries), and articles of iron or steel (HS73, 11 countries). The major products imported from India are not identical: pharmaceutical products (HS30, 22 countries), cereals (HS10, 10 countries), electrical (11 countries) and mechanical (13 countries) machinery and vehicles (15 countries) whilst iron or steel (9 countries) is more important than articles of iron or steel (Table 2.6). For 14 of the 24 SSA countries, at least two of these sectors are in the top four for China and India, i.e., to some extent they compete against each other in SSA import markets. In general these products will not compete with local industries; South Africa may be the exception for vehicles, machinery and pharmaceutical products that have high import shares (Table A8).

Certain Chinese imports in some countries are likely to compete with local producers. Examples of this include furniture (HS94, in Burundi, Cape Verde, Namibia and Seychelles), footwear (HS64, Malawi, South Africa and Uganda), ceramic products (HS69, Cape Verde and Nigeria), soap (HS34, The Gambia) and apparel (HS62, Sudan) (see Table A8). Imports of such products are likely to be present in other countries, but not in the top four import categories. Thus, there are likely to be simple manufactures and consumer goods where China, and increasingly India, competes with local producers. To assess this would, however, require analysis at a detailed individual country level.

A final observation here is that China and India account for significant shares of cotton imports for The Gambia and Mauritius (Table A8; combined shares are 28 per cent and 17 per cent respectively). This is an indication of situations where China and India provide textiles (or processed cotton) as an input to garments production in SSA countries, which is likely to be related to investment by Chinese and Indian firms (perhaps motivated by preferential access to the EU and US markets).

Summary and conclusions

As in most issues concerning Africa, it is unhelpful to think of SSA as an aggregate in terms of the implications of trade with China and India. A number of SSA countries that export minerals, especially oil, have trade surpluses with China. Overall, African trade is largely balanced (UNCTAD, 2010: 31). However, a number of SSA countries may face increasing trade deficits with China or India: the commodities they export are not in significant demand, whereas imports are increasing. In many cases the imports displace suppliers in the rest of the world, but in other cases, such as consumer goods, they compete with domestic producers.

In terms of exports to China and India, eight resource-rich SSA countries dominate and hence are the main beneficiaries. Although South Africa is the only country with some capacity to export manufactures, a number of SSA countries could expand their exports to China and India of soft commodities such as coffee, cocoa, tobacco; fruits, nuts and vegetables; oils and resins (especially to India); and potentially seafood. Timber and cotton exports are also significant for a few countries. Thus, although in value terms exports are highly concentrated, many SSA countries have opportunities.

Imports are also concentrated in value terms, with South Africa and Nigeria accounting for more than half of the value of SSA imports from China and India. However, there are increasing import shares in many SSA countries. China accounts for over 10 per cent of imports for seven countries, and over 20 per cent for two. India had a larger import share than China in a number of SSA countries mostly on or close to the Indian Ocean that have an expatriate Indian business community.

China and India have their largest import shares for industrial goods such as electrical and mechanical machinery and equipment, vehicles, iron and steel, and for India also pharmaceutical products and cereals. In these products they are likely to be displacing suppliers from the rest of the world. China is more likely than India at present to provide imports such as furniture, footwear and ceramic products that compete with local producers. In some cases China and India have significant shares of textiles imports for the garment sector (in which they may have invested).

It can be seen from this review that trade with China and India affects SSA countries differently as in general the countries that export the most to China and India are not the same as the countries with the greatest import penetration. More specifically, from an import perspective, the issue is whether cheap imports are competing with domestic producers. These issues can only be fully analysed at a country level. This is beyond the scope of this report although we have indicated the issues to address.

Notes

1.   The Harmonized System (HS), developed and maintained by the World Customs Organization, is used to classify commodities. The first two digits (HS2) identify the chapter the goods are classified in. See Annex Table A.1 for a detailed list of HS2 categories.

3

Investment and Aid Relationships

Whereas reasonably good data are available to demonstrate the importance of China and India in terms of trade, data on capital flows are more limited. In parallel with its rise as a trading partner – largely because the trade opportunities create investment opportunities – aid and investment flows from China to SSA have increased significantly in recent years. There is sufficient information on foreign direct investment (FDI) to show the increasing importance of China, and to a lesser extent India, in Africa (see UNCTAD, 2010, Chapter 4). However, consolidated data on 'aid to Africa' do not exist; concessional flows are often closely linked to trade or investment so that levels of aid are hard to determine. Nevertheless, capital flows of various forms to Africa are increasing.

World FDI stock, measured as outward or inward, has increased some 14 times between 1982–1990 and 2005–2008 (UNCTAD, 2009). Although developed economies dominate FDI as hosts and sources, their relative importance in terms of inward and outward FDI flows and stocks has declined over time. The combined stock held by the G7 major industrial countries fell from an average of 79 per cent of world outward FDI stock during 1982–1999 to 55 per cent during 2005–2008 (UNCTAD, 2009). As the relative importance of the major industrial countries declined, China's position (and India's to a limited degree) increased steadily. Greater China (mainland China, Hong Kong and Taiwan) ranked as the fifth largest source of world outward FDI stock during 2005–2008, with an average share of 6.8 per cent, while India was 31st accounting for an average share of 0.2 per cent (UNCTAD, 2009). However, it is the pace at which China (outward FDI from US$1.7 billion during 1982–1990 to US$93.6 billion during 2005–2008) and India (outward FDI from US$99 million during 1982–1990 to US$35.7 billion during 2005–2008) have increased their FDI portfolio and also the scale and speed of penetration into some parts of the developing world (including SSA) that is notable. Thus although from a global perspective China's and India's investments abroad remain relatively low, they are increasingly important in SSA.

China's surge of outward FDI is a relatively recent phenomenon following reforms and deliberate policies under the 'Going Global Strategy' to secure natural resources to fuel rapid growth and, equally important, business opportunities in the service industry. Under this strategy the Chinese Government encourages qualified enterprises to go abroad and engage in multinational operations to achieve mutual development. The result is clearly discernible as Chinese investments abroad doubled each year between 2004 and 2008. According to the WTO (2010), by the end of 2009 Chinese enterprises had established 18 overseas economic and trade co-operation zones in 14 countries to facilitate outbound investment. Some three-quarters of total Chinese outward FDI was in business services, financial sectors, wholesale and retail (ibid.: Table I.10). India's outward FDI flows followed a similar trend, albeit at much lower levels.

FDI and investment in SSA

Although the SSA share of world inward FDI stock fell from 2.9 per cent to 2.2 per cent during 2005–2008, FDI stock in SSA has grown from US$31 billion during 1982–1990 to US$266 billion over the same period (Appendix Table A11). To a large extent this spectacular growth was driven by inflows from China and India. 'Indian investments (outward stock) in Africa amounted to some US$2.7 billion in 2008, compared to US$7.8 billion for China' (UNCTAD, 2010: Figure 7). The major beneficiaries were mineral rich countries including Angola, Nigeria, South Africa and Sudan – it is notable that these are the same countries that export to China and India. Over 2005–2008, South Africa accounted for almost 1 per cent of global inward FDI stock, over a third of the SSA stock; Nigeria accounted for over a fifth of the SSA stock while Angola and Sudan accounted for 5 per cent (Table A12). Other countries that export to China and India, notably Equatorial Guinea and Zambia, are also among the largest SSA recipients of FDI.

There is widespread recognition that Chinese investment in SSA is now significant. Furthermore, because the focus of this investment is on resource extraction to feed China's demand for oil and mineral imports, there is concern that Chinese behaviour may be similar to that of (Western) multinationals historically, i.e., SSA countries may not be getting the 'best' price for their resources. Against this, a less widely recognised factor is the competition between Chinese firms investing in Africa. For example, the China National Petroleum Corporation (CNPC) and the China Petroleum and Chemical Corporation (Sinopec) competed with each other over an oil pipeline project in Sudan (Taylor, 2010: 7).

SAA countries experienced dramatic growth in FDI inflows at an annual average rate of 16 per cent over 2000–2004 and 28 per cent over 2005–2008; although small countries such as São Tomé and Principe or Equatorial Guinea that discovered resources had the largest increases, the growth is spread across most countries (except Botswana, whose stock of FDI fell) (Table A13). Although FDI to SSA averaged less than 2 per cent of total global inward FDI flows during 1982–2008, the growth rate into SSA was twice the global growth in the second half of the 2000s, reflecting flows from China and India. Eight countries account for over 80 per cent of inward FDI flows to SSA: in order of importance, Nigeria, Angola, South Africa, Sudan, Congo, Equatorial Guinea, Ghana and Zambia (Table A14) – only Ghana is not among the eight major exporters to China and India. The top four countries alone accounted for 59 per cent of all FDI inflows to SSA during 1982–2004 and increased their share to 64 per cent during 2005–2008, while the other four major recipients accounted for 9 per cent and 12 per cent during 1982–2004 and 2005–2008, respectively.

The relative importance of global FDI (stock and flows) for SSA countries is revealed where FDI is expressed as a share of GDP. Total FDI stock was equivalent to 15 per cent of SSA GDP over 2002–2008, although this had risen to 22 per cent in 2008 and was about 26 per cent of GDP for the average country (Table A15). For Equatorial Guinea (where there appears to be an error), Liberia, Seychelles (a tax haven) and Congo the FDI stock exceeded GDP. Perhaps of greater importance is that total FDI inflows increased from 1.2 per cent of SSA GDP in 2002 to 4.1 per cent in 2008 (Table A16). For major recipients, inflows account for significant shares of GDP, averaging over 20 per cent of GDP during 2002–2008 for Angola, Congo and Equatorial Guinea, for example, and over 5 per cent of GDP in 2008 for 16 countries (Table A16).

Table 3.1. Chinese and world FDI stock in SSA, 1990 and 2005

		Chinese FDI (US$)		World FDI (US$)		China/World %	
		1990	2005	1990	2005	1990	2005
	SSA	33.0	1,305.1	36,746.0	194,545.3	0.1	0.7
1	Sudan		351.5	55.3	7,684.1	0.0	4.6
2	Zambia	3.2	160.3	2,655.5	5,409.0	0.1	3.0
3	South Africa		112.3	9,207.2	78,984.5	0.0	0.1
4	Nigeria	6.7	94.1	8,538.6	36,380.7	0.1	0.3
5	United Rep. of Tanzania	1.7	62.0	387.8	4,390.0	0.4	1.4
6	Kenya	0.5	58.3	667.9	1,113.3	0.1	5.2
7	Madagascar	1.7	49.9	106.8	250.3	1.6	19.9
8	Guinea		44.2	68.8	580.7	0.0	7.6
9	Zimbabwe	2.5	41.6	277.1	1,383.1	0.9	3.0
10	Gabon	2.9	35.4	1,208.4	488.4	0.2	7.2
11	Ethiopia		29.8	..	2,820.8	..	1.1
12	Côte d'Ivoire	0.6	29.1	975.4	3,901.3	0.1	0.7
13	Mauritius	6.3	26.8	167.8	804.7	3.8	3.3
14	DR Congo		25.1	546.4	908.3	0.0	2.8
15	Niger	0.1	20.4	286.4	100.0	0.0	20.4
16	Sierra Leone	1.1	18.4	243.1	304.0	0.5	6.1
17	Botswana	0.0	18.1	1,309.3	806.3	0.0	2.2
18	Equatorial Guinea		16.6	25.4	7,362.6	0.0	0.2
19	Liberia		15.9	2,731.6	3,788.0	0.0	0.4
20	Mozambique	0.1	14.7	24.8	2,630.0	0.4	0.6
21	Congo		13.3	575.2	2,912.6	0.0	0.5
22	Mali	0.0	13.3	229.4	871.6	0.0	1.5
23	Angola		8.8	1,024.4	12,132.9	0.0	0.1
24	Cameroon	0.5	7.9	1,044.0	3,202.2	0.0	0.2
25	Ghana		7.3	319.3	2,142.9	0.0	0.3
26	Uganda		5.0	6.0	2,024.4	0.0	0.2
27	Togo	0.2	4.8	268.0	713.8	0.1	0.7
28	Rwanda	2.9	4.7	32.7	77.0	8.9	6.1
29	Seychelles		4.2	212.9	808.5	0.0	0.5
30	Chad	0.1	2.7	249.7	3,040.0	0.0	0.1
31	Namibia		2.4	2,046.8	2,453.4	0.0	0.1
32	Senegal	0.2	2.4	258.3	358.2	0.1	0.7
33	C. African Rep.	1.2	2.0	95.4	198.3	1.3	1.0
34	Gambia	0.5	1.2	156.6	372.5	0.3	0.3
35	Cape Verde		0.6	3.8	360.9	0.0	0.2

Source: Data on Chinese FDI stock in SSA countries taken from UNCTAD (2006) as reported by Besada (2008: 18). Data on World FDI stock in SSA taken from UNCTAD (2009).

Chinese FDI stock held in SSA is shown in Table 3.1, where mineral-rich countries such as Nigeria, South Africa, Sudan and Zambia have been the major targets. However, the stock of Chinese FDI is also relatively high in countries such as Kenya, Madagascar and United Republic of Tanzania. As this reports 2005 values it may reflect investment in the garment sector. In relation to the total (world) FDI stock in individual SSA countries, Chinese FDI stock is very small except in Madagascar and Niger where it represents 20 per cent of total FDI stock.

What is also clear for all those SSA countries where data are available is the considerable increase in Chinese FDI stock. Over the past few years this has risen sharply under China's foreign co-operation programme in relation to contracted engineering projects, labour services and design consultation services (Kragelund and van Dijk, 2009). The changes in the shares of Chinese FDI stock from 1990 to 2005 (as indicated in Table 3.1) are noteworthy. However, because the data end in 2005 they miss more recent increases, which in some cases are likely to be significant (Angola in particular, and possibly also Equatorial Guinea). Current data would be likely to show the rise of resource rich countries to the top of the list of recipients.

Chinese FDI to African countries reflects closer economic ties. 'The leading African recipient of FDI from China is South Africa followed by Nigeria, Zambia, Sudan, Algeria, Mauritius, United Republic of Tanzania, Madagascar, Niger, Congo, Egypt and Ethiopia' (UNCTAD, 2010: 84). Although Chinese FDI goes mostly to those SSA countries from which it imports, Indian FDI has a more historic pattern: accumulated flows to Mauritius (US$1.4 billion during 1996–2005) accounted for 9 per cent of total outward FDI; only recently has India had large investment in other countries such as Côte d'Ivoire, Senegal and Sudan (UNCTAD, 2010: 86).

The growing relative importance of China and India as sources of FDI for SSA is seen in the amounts involved, the speed of FDI growth, the relatively soft terms involved and the broad coverage of beneficiary countries. The driving motivation behind some of China's FDI (especially by state-owned enterprises) transcends the profit maximisation objectives of multinationals from developed countries. Instead FDI by Chinese state-owned enterprises that enjoy access to low-cost capital at home tends to be driven by the objective of establishing strategic long-term relationships, often intended to secure access to mineral resources for Chinese industries (Besada, 2008: 19). Although Chinese investment in Africa is concentrated in extractive industries and agriculture, 'Chinese firms are also taking on a significant number of manufacturing, construction and infrastructure projects (often ones considered too risky by European or US firms). In Sierra Leone in 2005 – within two years of the end of the civil war – China invested US$270 million in hotel construction and tourism' (OECD, 2010: 83).

Factors that have helped the rapid expansion of Chinese FDI in recent times include heavily subsidised capital available to enterprises seeking to invest abroad; relaxed requirements for the state-owned enterprises to adopt internationally recognised standards; the use of materials directly imported from China, and the almost exclusive use of relatively cheap Chinese labour (Besada, 2008: 22). China also invests in the textiles and clothing sectors, thus availing of SSA trade preferences to avoid US and European limits on Chinese textile and clothing exports.

Indian FDI is directed mostly to countries in South and East Asia, often linked to regional trade and integration. Mauritius has also been a beneficiary. Some of this is 'round-tripping' investment (UNCTAD, 2004), i.e., domestic investment routed through Mauritius back into India to take advantage of fiscal incentives accorded foreign investment, although some is likely to reflect established investment in the garment sector. Sudan is the only other SSA country in the top 30 recipients of Indian outward FDI, absorbing 9 per cent of this between 1996 and 2003 (DFID, 2005: 32).

Data on the scale of Chinese FDI in SSA should be interpreted with caution given the measurement difficulties; Chinese activity in SSA may be FDI, winning commercial tenders, part of a Chinese aid package or joint ventures between Chinese and SSA firms. Fewer than 50 investments in SSA per annum were recorded by the Chinese Ministry of Commerce between 1998 and 2002 (Kaplinsky *et al.*, 2006: 14). Anecdotal evidence suggests a large increase in Chinese enterprises undertaking large projects (e.g., construction or rehabilitation of infrastructure, such as roads in Mozambique), but there are many small-scale initiatives including distribution (wholesale and retail of Chinese goods, e.g., in Namibia and Zambia) and light manufacturing (e.g., manufacture of mattresses, tiles and hair lotions under a joint venture with the Sierra Leone Government). Between 1998 and 2002, Chinese FDI in Africa tended to be in relatively small scale with an average portfolio size of less than US$3 million.

An increasing number of large Chinese energy firms (such as CNPC and Sinopec) have invested in SSA, especially oil projects in Angola, Gabon, Nigeria and Sudan. Most of these are wholly or partly state-owned and enjoy financial support in the form of soft loans and/or grants. For example, CNPC invested heavily in Sudan under a joint venture arrangement with the Sudanese Government and other foreign energy firms, has a 40 per cent stake in the Greater Nile Petroleum Operating Company and has an equivalent stake in another project in Darfur and Melut Basin. Backed by the state, CNPC is also a big investor in Nigeria for oil exploration, construction of a 1,000-megawatt hydroelectric plant in Mambila and a controlling share of a refinery in Kaduna. Sinopec has large investments in Angola, Gabon and Sudan. Chinese firms have also invested in the mining of copper in Zambia and cobalt in Democratic Republic of the Congo.

Large Chinese construction corporations are also involved in the construction and/or rehabilitation of infrastructure across SSA. Typical projects include sports stadiums, presidential palaces (Kinshasa), dams, roads, railways, parliaments and government buildings (Mozambique) and conference centres (Mozambique). Kaplinsky *et al.* (2006) list the factors underlying the growing participation of Chinese firms in construction and infrastructure projects in SSA as: low margins; access to cheaper capital than local investors (a gap of 15 per cent according to Manchester Trade Team, 2005); almost exclusive use of low-paid Chinese labour and construction materials; the use of standard designs; low attention to environmental standards; and access to subsidies and hard currency through the Chinese Government. 'Evidence suggests that Chinese investors conduct most of their business with government agencies and purchase a substantial share of their inputs from China. This has adverse consequences for the creation of linkages between Chinese FDI and host economies in the region' (UNCTAD, 2010: 84).

Chinese and Indian aid

It is difficult to quantify how much aid China and India give to Africa as they do not adopt the definitions of aid employed by the DAC, do not have a single aid agency and often closely link concessional flows to trade or investment (such as export credits and lines of credit). On the basis of information on official concessional flows, UNCTAD (2010: 53) estimates that in 2006 China gave some US$2.3 billion in aid (US$1.3 billion of which was debt relief) to Africa and India gave about US$11 million. Katti *et al.* (2009: 2) estimate Indian aid to Africa as varying from US$14 million in 2005–2006, US$4 million on 2006–2007 and US$11 million in 2007–2008. Whatever the true value, official flows from India are clearly much smaller than those from China.

China does not provide data on the amount of aid it gives, in total or to individual countries, although it is evident that the amount has grown significantly over the past decade, with a concentration in Africa. Although most SSA countries receive aid from China, Angola, Congo, Nigeria, Sudan and Zambia are the major beneficiaries (UNCTAD, 2010: 55), highlighting the link to resources (all five of these are among the top exporters to China). India also concentrates aid on countries that export to it – Nigeria and Sudan are the major recipients of infrastructure investment, although credits are spread over a number of West African countries (ibid.). For both China and India the aid is more likely to be in the form of concessional loans rather than grants, concentrated in infrastructure or projects related to trade.

The literature focuses on three features of Chinese aid to Africa (Chaponniere, 2009; Lancaster, 2007): (1) it is linked to commercial interest, in particular access to oil, mineral and timber resources; (2) it is typically invested in large infrastructure projects (often transport and related to resource extraction, but including schools and medical facilities); and (3) it is not associated with the types of policy or governance conditions advocated by Western donors. The last of these makes Chinese aid attractive to SSA governments: 'low conditionality combined with the project-based approach of Chinese aid provides a useful alternative model for the donor community – albeit with its own drawbacks and limitations (e.g., a lack of transparency, a high share of tied-aid)' (OECD, 2010: 89). While the unwillingness to engage with policy and governance issues may undermine efforts to ensure that the aid (and associated foreign investment) contributes to development, it should be acknowledged that both China and India espouse principles of partnership and mutual support in their aid.

Another important feature of Chinese aid is that it is highly tied, not only to Chinese firms for construction and materials but even including Chinese labour. In fact, the Chinese firms that get entry to SSA countries through aid projects tend to remain in the country, setting up a local office and retaining the equipment they have brought in so that they are locally very competitive (Taylor, 2010: 23). On this basis Chinese aid, as compared to other donors, can be criticised as offering fewer local linkages and hence less benefit to local private sector firms and employment. However, Besada (2008) notes that Chinese aid is also allocated to building low-cost housing, schools and sports stadiums; provision of doctors and humanitarian aid; and scholarships for Africans to study in China.

It seems appropriate to consider much of Chinese aid and investment (and perhaps also debt relief) as parts of a strategy for gaining access to a supply of important raw materials.

For example, China offered Angola US$2 billion in aid in 2005 subject to the condition that it has a right to 10,000 barrels of oil per day (Taylor, 2010: 20–21). This need not be to the detriment of SSA countries, as long as the resource extraction sector provides revenue to the government (to support development objectives) as well as linkages and employment to the domestic economy. Although current volumes are much lower, India is strengthening its ties with Africa through lines of credit, FDI and technical assistance (Katti *et al.*, 2009: 1). India also promotes private sector co-operation and investment in Africa, such as investment by the state-owned Oil and Natural Gas Company in Nigeria and Sudan (ibid.: 2).

Kaplinsky *et al.* (2006: 22) classify Chinese economic aid to SSA into five categories: (1) infrastructure projects, e.g., rehabilitation of the 1,860km TAZARA railway linking Dar es Salaam and Zambia (passing through Zambia's copper-belt region); (2) debt relief, although debts to China have rarely been large; (3) academic scholarships for Africans to study in China; (4) technical assistance in health (doctors) and agriculture (e.g., rice production in Malawi); and (5) provision of preferential (duty free) market access. The latter, effective since 2005 for selected products (including food, textiles, minerals and light machinery) may have been important in facilitating the growth of non-mineral exports to China as previously SSA exports faced high tariffs (above 30 per cent). This could be seen as a Chinese interpretation of aid for trade. Nevertheless, most aid in value terms is allocated to infrastructure and likely to be linked to investment.

The increased official flows from China have relaxed resource constraints in SSA countries and provided a valuable alternative to traditional (Western) donors. 'There are a number of potential benefits from Chinese aid: better targeting on important infrastructure projects with long maturity and long-term potential; less bureaucracy (meaning lower transaction costs), greater efficiency and potentially faster response; and [less policy] conditionality' (OECD, 2010: 89). China is likely to become even more important as a source of aid and investment in the future, so the challenge for African countries is how to make the best use of the flexibility provided.

India is also likely to become a more important source of aid and investment, given the commitments made at the India–Africa Forum Summit in 2008 (Katti *et al.*, 2009: 4). India promised to allocate some US$1 billion each year in lines of credit over five years, mostly for irrigation and agricultural production, food processing, infrastructure and energy, information technology and pharmaceuticals. This will be supplemented with grants of US$500 million for human resource development and capacity building.

Conclusions and implications

China has become a major aid and investment partner for many SSA countries, especially those that are a source of mineral resources. In general, it is investing in the same mineral-rich SSA countries that attract global FDI. Indian FDI has historically been concentrated in manufacturing, especially garments, and retail and hotel services, especially in Mauritius, but is also diversifying (including into Sudan – the prime example of a country shunned by the West but attractive to China and India).

The flow and accumulation of Chinese and Indian investments in SSA has been accompanied by substantial increases in Chinese and Indian migrant workers and traders. These workers follow the aid and grant-aided infrastructure and social capital development programmes including in the construction, health and education sectors. By some counts the population of Chinese migrant workers in Lusaka, for example, increased tenfold from 3,000 in 1995 to 30,000 in 2005, and 200,000 Chinese (the majority recent migrants) lived in South Africa in 2005 (Kaplinsky, 2007: 7). The migration of Indians into SSA started in the late nineteenth century and continues to date. Most Indians in SSA engage in the distribution (wholesale and retail) service sector, largely in the eastern and southern countries bordering the Indian Ocean.

These observations highlight the inter-linked nature of Chinese aid and investment; although not well documented, similar issues appear to apply to India. In many cases aid is used in effect to subsidise investments, either directly as part of the investment finance or indirectly by supporting related infrastructure projects. For example, building and rehabilitating roads supports the transport of extracted resources. This is in addition to subsidies that Chinese firms often receive for foreign investment. This need not reduce the benefits to SSA countries, but it does make it difficult, and perhaps irrelevant, to try and distinguish aid and investment.

The more potentially damaging aspect of Chinese projects, whether aid or investment, is their tied nature – Chinese capital goods, inputs and even labour are all used (this may in part explain the large share in machinery imports). Furthermore, once the firms enter with materials and labour for a project, they use this to establish themselves in the local economy. At a minimum this reduces the potential linkages with the local economy as local suppliers are not supported. In some cases it may damage the local economy as it displaces local suppliers and labour (given that unskilled labour is abundant in SSA). Chinese aid and investment have delivered benefits to SSA countries, but there are many reasons to believe that these are less that they could be.

As investment and aid from China and India are linked and often involve firms, they offer potential for private sector development. 'Partnerships between African and Chinese firms may facilitate technology transfer, add value to African exports, and help African firms position themselves to benefit from world markets – not least the rapidly expanding Chinese market … [experience with India] shows that these clusters need not be restricted to manufacturing. Certain services including ICTs, financial services or tourism can enhance the generating of dynamic clusters (OECD, 2010: 142).

A final point to note is that the increase in FDI into China and India is unlikely to displace FDI to SSA (DFID, 2005: 35) as a large proportion comes from within the Asian region (Gottschalk, 2005; Rumbaugh and Blancher, 2004). According to UNCTAD (2003: 45) overseas Chinese are behind most of the regional FDI flow back into their homeland; overseas Indians are fewer and invest less into India. Furthermore, FDI into China and India is in high productive export sectors and services (information and communication technology, banking and finance).

4

Future Prospects and Policy Options

As the previous sections have indicated, the growth of China and India has affected SSA through various linkages including trade, foreign direct investment (FDI), aid and debt relief, and migration of Chinese and Indian workers. The impacts are both complementary and competitive, and direct and indirect. The growth of these two countries stimulated demand for raw materials, oil and other intermediate inputs for their domestic markets and export-oriented industries. Because of their relative economic mass, that demand has translated into a general global rise in input prices of the affected commodities. Trade is therefore the principal channel through which the growth of China and India has had an impact on the global economy in general and SSA in particular. Trade opportunities have also influenced Chinese FDI in SSA to secure supplies of resource inputs.

The report has shown that there are two broad categories of SSA countries: mineral resource-rich exporters, which have a clear opportunity to benefit from a dynamic economic partnership with emerging economies; and other SSA countries, which have fewer export opportunities and face challenges from declining preference margins for their exports and increased competition from imports (especially from China and India). The discussion here will focus on China, as being currently the more important partner for which more data are available. As the SSA countries that export to India, and the products, are similar the same observations apply (we will note possible differences in potential export diversification). It is also true that there is similarity between the most important products imported from China and India, although again we will note differences. Mayer and Fajarnes (2008) are optimistic about the potential for SSA primary exports to benefit from a further rise in Chinese demand and the subsequent growth in Indian demand. However, while no more than 10 SSA countries account for almost all exports to China and India, the importance of Chinese and Indian imports is dispersed across most SSA countries. Nigeria and South Africa account for about half (and are also major exporters), but there are significant imports in many other countries – notably Ethiopia, Ghana, Kenya, Madagascar, Mauritius, Sudan and Uganda (of these only Sudan is a major exporter to China). Thus there is a significant differential impact on SSA countries, largely depending on what they produce and export.

Another important distinction is between LDCs and non-LDCs. As noted earlier, the same eight SSA countries are the major exporters to China and India: five of these are LDCs (Guillaumont, 2009: 6–7) – Angola, Democratic Republic of the Congo, Equatorial Guinea, Sudan and Zambia – while Nigeria and South Africa are non-LDCs; Congo is not classed as an LDC.[1] Thus, the 28 other SSA LDCs are not (sufficient) mineral exporters to benefit significantly from demand from China and India. Many of them are exporters of soft (agriculture) commodities so there is potential to avail of the preferential (tariff-free) access granted by China and India; in this they have an advantage over SSA non-LDCs, such as Ghana and Kenya, that export similar products but without the same preferences (except in access to the EU and to the US under the African Growth Opportunity Act, AGOA). This is potentially important: as LDCs have received the largest trade preferences they are the most vulnerable to preference erosion; only three SSA non-LDCs face significant preference erosion – Côte d'Ivoire (for bananas), Mauritius (for sugar) and Seychelles (for fish) (Milner et al., 2010: 38). While in respect of exports, China and India offer more opportunities to LDCs than to non-LDCs, in respect of imports there is little distinction. Although non-LDCs are more likely to have import-competing producers and to import more, many LDCs also import significant amounts from China and India.

The strategy for responding to China and India should recognise the context of recent SSA experience with trade and trade reform. In the past two decades, most SSA countries liberalised their trade regime, many greatly reducing restrictions on imports; evidence for this can be found in lower average tariffs and, perhaps more significantly, in increases in imports as a share of GDP. Multilateral (WTO) and regional (especially with the EU) agreements have committed them to these reforms. To date, there is little aggregate evidence that these trade policy reforms have produced a significant export response (Morrissey, 2005); exports have not increased consistently, and there is no evident correlation between the extent of trade liberalisation and the rate at which exports have grown (increases in global commodity prices remain the major determinant of increases in export revenue for SSA countries). Export diversification requires additional policies to provide incentives to induce a shift into new export commodities (the common problem here is in identifying 'new' commodities that may in future be internationally competitive) or expand the capacity to produce traditional exports (constrained by limited supply response). However, export diversification has been very limited with the exception of a few countries (e.g., horticulture in Kenya) and 'new' exports have often simply reflected discoveries of minerals (e.g., gold in United Republic of Tanzania). On the other hand, cheaper imports have increased the competition faced by domestic import-competing producers, although consumers (including producers importing capital goods and intermediate inputs) have benefited.

The structure of SSA exports is a particular problem. SSA countries' relative endowments of land and natural resources result in export dependency on primary commodities, and few countries are significant exporters of manufactures (Mauritius and South Africa being the major exceptions). While demand from China and India has been helpful in increasing earnings for mineral exporters, it has done little so far to support other commodity exports or to promote diversification. Dependence on primary commodities subjects exports to the vagaries of a volatile world market; exports also tend to be relatively bulky with high volume-to-price ratios. Many SSA countries are landlocked and many of those that are not have large interiors. Transporting the primary commodities they produce tends to be expensive since these have to be transported large distances overland to reach ports, road and rail systems are often inefficient and sea shipping costs are relatively high (Milner et al., 2000). In such a situation, trade confers limited benefits – the capacity of the export sector to respond is impeded, whereas domestic producers will face increased competition from imports.

In countries dependent on agricultural exports, farmers face many constraints in gaining access to factors, inputs and technology, which restricts their ability to increase production in response to improved (export) price incentives (Morrissey, 2005). Consequently, one rarely observes a quick export response to higher prices or new market opportunities. Domestic policies are necessary to reduce the varied constraints on supply response, increase transport and marketing efficiency and encourage investment in transport, distribution, business services and trade facilitation. SSA countries need to increase the flexibility and efficiency of resource use so that they can be competitive in global markets. The inflexibility of factor markets, a serious problem in Africa, is a major impediment to gaining from trade as it limits the ability to reallocate resources. The ability of SSA countries to expand exports of manufactures is severely restricted by the small size and low levels of efficiency and of investment in technology of local manufacturing firms.

Whilst it is useful to consider exports to and imports from China and India separately it must be acknowledged that both countries can affect the pattern of SSA trade, within SSA as well as export shares in world products, and the types of products traded. Kaplinsky and Morris (2008, especially Table 9) consider the technology-intensity of SSA trade. As previously noted, SSA exports to China are mostly primary commodities (oil and gas, accounting for 81 per cent) or resource-based (15 per cent), while the pattern of exports to India is reversed with resource-based products (46 per cent) a greater share than primary commodities (38 per cent). These two categories also account for over 80 per cent of SSA exports to the rest of the world. Thus, extra-regional exports are largely unprocessed, i.e., can be considered as having no technology-intensity (although extraction is capital intensive, there is no manufacturing technology). The main implication is that few SSA exports generate significant value-added or promote production linkages and technology spillovers with the rest of the economy.

Addressing this (long-standing) problem requires SSA countries to move into processing activities, i.e., some of the manufacturing that adds value to the primary resources they have. This would be in medium technology manufactures, in which there is some activity (low technology goods tend be labour intensive and SSA is not competitive given high labour costs, especially relative to Asia). Although resource-based products account for 35 per cent of intra-SSA exports, medium technology products, which have the highest share in intra-SSA markets compared to other markets, account for 23 per cent (Kaplinsky and Morris, 2008, Table 9). Generally, the relatively technology-intensive SSA exports can compete with similar products within SSA (enjoying preferential market access and advantages of proximity) even if SSA manufactures are not competitive against similar products from more efficient global producers on the global markets. Regional trade, and by implication regional integration, offers the best opportunity to promote manufactures exports in SSA.

Growth in exports of low-cost manufactures by China and India has been accompanied by substantial declines in world manufacturing prices (Kaplinsky et al., 2006). This poses a serious threat of China and India crowding out SSA's small range of manufactures exports in third-country markets and also out-competing SSA manufacturers in their domestic markets. As discussed in Section 2, the clothing sector may be the best example of this (see also below). While SSA countries should not neglect opportunities to develop garment exports, these may not be a secure platform for long-term export growth. Thus, the basic message in terms of a development-oriented long-term SSA export strategy is to concentrate on adding value (processing) to the resources they have.

Opportunities for SSA

As they are predominantly exporters of primary commodities, one of the most important stylised facts for SSA is the trend decline in commodity prices throughout most of the last century for the goods they export; only recently has a reversal been evident, mostly for minerals. Between 1990 and 2000 world prices for cocoa, cotton, sugar and copper declined by over 25 per cent, coffee by 9 per cent and minerals overall by 14 per cent (WTO, 2001: 212). Producers responded to this; in particular, farmers tended to diversify away from traditional (cash crop) exports towards food crops for the domestic market. However, given various problems afflicting agriculture, food production rarely kept pace with population growth. Commodity prices surged during 2001–2008, fuelled by demand from China: for Africa as a whole, export unit prices fell by 2 per cent per annum between 1995 and 2001, but increased at a rate of 17 per cent per annum between 2002 and 2006 (UNCTAD, 2008).

For those countries that are already exporting raw materials to China and India, and for others that discover or develop extractive resources in the future, the issue is ensuring that the sector benefits the whole economy and generates investment to support diversification. For SSA countries that lack mineral resources, the issue is accessing markets in China and India for what they can export. For example, there is potential for food exports in the longer term (as China and India account for some 40 per cent of world population). The two types of country are considered separately, but an export diversification strategy is considered in a common framework covering three inter-linked issues: (1) ensuring domestic revenue from export earnings; (2) ensuring a development impact from investment projects; and (3) promoting local linkages.

Exports of mineral resource-rich countries

As observed above, the major commodities exported by SSA to China and India are mineral fuels, ores, stones and metals in value terms. The mineral resource-rich SSA countries that export these products should focus on how to benefit most from the opportunity presented by a dynamic economic partnership. As China and India are likely to sustain their growth for a considerable period, even if at lower rates, the markets are reasonably secure and steady demand for a volume of exports can be anticipated. The concern for the SSA countries essentially relates to the price, or more generally the share of the export value retained in the exporting economy. There is no reason to believe that this share is high or even reasonable as typically foreign firms are involved in extraction and export (in this respect, Chinese firms are no different to Western multinationals), and the price or rent received by the country is negotiated between the firm and host government (and costly corruption cannot be discounted).

A number of principles can be advanced to guide negotiating, or renegotiating, the revenue received (typically a payment from the multinational to the government). First, even if a forward price is specified the world price should be a reference. A suitable aim is that the government receives a proportion of the world price such that the value of this proportion is greater than a minimum price per unit exported. Export revenue rises in line with prices, but should the world price fall the government is guaranteed the threshold price. Second, the government should designate a fund in which the revenue is placed and indicate how the revenue will be spent or invested (where the revenue involved is very large, a Sovereign Wealth Fund is appropriate). Transparency is desirable so the allocation of revenue, in particular any contribution to government expenditure, can be monitored. Third, in the case of large projects, the investor should provide some investment in development (e.g., hospitals, schools or sanitation for affected local communities); this could be considered as an offset against any investment incentives (such as tax breaks) but not against the price. Finally, the investor should commit to employ local labour insofar as possible, at least for less skilled work, and where local input or service suppliers exist they should have the opportunity to tender in an open process. This final set of principles can be applied to any large investment (or aid) project as a means of promoting local linkages to benefit the economy.

Exports of soft commodities

It is evident that SSA countries are increasing exports to China and India for a variety of soft (agricultural) commodities, such as cotton, coffee, cocoa, tobacco; fruits, nuts and vegetables; and oils and resins. Some SSA countries may be able to export seafood, and others have potential in hides, timber and wood pulp. Countries that have production capacity in these products should be given some assistance in identifying the potential for exports to China and India. Note that these are typically products in which SSA countries already have (potential) comparative advantage so they are sectors suitable for policy support anyway. Although investment is needed to increase productivity, and foreign investment may be suitable if it provides integration with global supply chains and access to technology, these are sectors particularly suited for domestic investment.

A particular problem facing SSA exporters of soft commodities is that the dynamics of global demand and prices are more complicated than for minerals. 'Agricultural commodities seem to have other drivers [compared to minerals ... D]emand from China, India or other emerging markets [has not been] an over-riding factor in determining price trends in this sector ... What is certain is that the huge populations of Brazil, China and India will mean these countries continue to play a critical role in world food markets as both major producers and consumers' (OECD, 2010: 51). This issue is most evident for food grains (and many SSA countries are net importers), where price volatility is caused by production shocks, such as associated with the recent fires in Russia and floods in Pakistan. Nevertheless, China and India represent new market opportunities.

Export diversification

History shows that resource-dependent exports have not generally supported African growth and development. Insofar as China and India (and other emerging markets) are merely displacing industrialised countries as export destinations, so that the commodity composition of trade is unaltered, the danger is that SSA countries are experiencing another commodity boom that will fizzle out, as previous booms have, without a lasting impact on development. To avoid the problems of the past and establish a platform for future growth, it is important to ensure that revenue from export earnings is invested in projects that promote linkages with the rest of the economy and support export diversification. A general strategy is to identify possibilities for value-added processing and the associated investment requirements, recognising that simply having the raw resource is not sufficient to justify establishing a processing sector. For example, processing of ores is typically energy-intensive, so it is only feasible to develop a processing sector if there is an adequate supply of electricity. Processing also requires a scale of activity to be efficient and competitive.

Given their access to trade preferences, LDCs have more opportunities than non-LDCs. The Duty Free Tariff Preference Scheme announced at the 2008 India–Africa Forum Summit provides opportunities for SSA LDCs to increase exports of minerals (aluminium and copper ores), soft commodities (such as cotton and cocoa), some foodstuffs (e.g., cashew nuts, cane sugar and fish) and even ready-made garments. Similar opportunities exist for China where LDCs also get tariff-free access for most products. The challenge for SSA LDCs is to produce the value-added products to benefit from these schemes.

Competition from China and India may also affect SSA exports to third countries. Quite detailed investigation and disaggregated data are required to determine where this may be the case. For example, although SSA may appear to compete in garments, it is rarely in head-to-head competition because countries can avail of trade preferences (and indeed China and India invest in SSA for this reason). It may also be that they produce different garments. To give another example, both Botswana and India export diamonds; however, closer investigation shows that Botswana exports raw diamonds while India exports cut diamonds. In this case Botswana and India are not competitors. It may be that India imports raw diamonds from Botswana to process and export as cut diamonds. The question for Botswana is whether it should engage in this processing. On the basis of highly disaggregated trade data, Kaplinsky and Santos Paulino (2006) find that increasing Chinese exports to the EU will tend to reduce prices, which will have an adverse impact on other low-income suppliers. However, these are more likely to be other countries in Asia rather than countries in SSA. Furthermore, as SSA producers (irrespective of whether or not they are LDCs) have preferential access to their main markets, the EU and USA, they are somewhat protected from competing with China and India.

In responding to trade relations with China and India, SSA needs to derive more benefit (especially revenue) from existing exports (mineral resources) and identify and diversify into new export opportunities. The former essentially relates to the terms on which access to resources is negotiated and export revenues are shared, typically done in conjunction with foreign investors, and the latter requires an investment strategy.

Indeed, any policies aimed at benefiting from trade opportunities should be linked to an economy-wide investment strategy.

Utilising official flows (FDI and aid)

Foreign investment in SSA has been driven largely by one of two motives (as most domestic markets are small, market serving is rarely a prime motive): access to resources (extractive industries), traditionally by multinationals aiming to serve world markets but recently by China ensuring supply to its own market; and export opportunities, in particular where SSA has preferential access to large markets (such as to the EU or USA, see Milner *et al.*, 2010). China (and probably India, although there is less information) has engaged in both types of investment in SSA. As relations with China and India develop, more investment is likely. As already mentioned, care is required to ensure that investment in extractive sectors generates real benefits for the local economy, and similar considerations apply for 'export-seeking' investment. SSA countries should be receptive to foreign investment that is offered, but they should ensure they get a full share of the benefits.

A particular problem with 'export-seeking' investment arises when it is attracted by temporary opportunities such as trade preferences. The experience of Chinese investment in the clothing sector shows how the benefits can be limited and transient. Prior to the late 1990s, Chinese clothing and textile firms were located in SSA to circumvent the Multi-Fibre Agreement (MFA), which placed quotas on Chinese (and other countries') exports of textiles and clothing (in particular to the USA). Since 2000, China has invested in clothing production in SSA to exploit the preferential market access to the USA under AGOA. Given these opportunities, the clothing and textiles sector in SSA expanded rapidly and became significant in some countries, e.g., garments were 99 per cent of Lesotho's total exports, 98 per cent of exports to the USA and 50 per cent of GDP in 2004 (Kaplinsky *et al.*, 2006, Table 2.5). Chinese FDI in clothing and textiles in Kenya's export processing zone (EPZ) saw the EPZ account for nearly 20 per cent of formal wage employment in 2003 (Kaplinsky *et al.*, 2006). However, Chinese firms imported intermediate inputs from China and engaged in limited investment in production facilities. The only significant case of the development of a clothing industry was the construction of a US$100 million denim plant in Lesotho, which started operations in mid-2004 (Kaplinsky *et al.*, 2006: 11). Although Chinese investment afforded host SSA countries an opportunity to participate in global value chains, few linkages (to local suppliers) were established to spread the benefits throughout the host economy.

The expiry of the MFA in January 2005 had the dramatic effect of increasing the relative significance of high costs of production in SSA, which had previously been outweighed by the advantages from circumventing the Agreement, so locations in Asia became more competitive. Chinese FDI started pulling out of some SSA countries, leading to declines in their garment exports and employment; the overnight gains of participating in global value chains disappeared with the deserting Chinese firms (Kaplinsky and Morris, 2008; 2009). The most affected countries were South Africa (where export value fell by 45 per cent), Lesotho (17 per cent) and Swaziland (10 per cent). Employment in the sector fell by

56.2 per cent in Swaziland, 28.9 per cent in Lesotho, 12.2 per cent in South Africa and 9.3 per cent in Kenya. Relations with China and India provide opportunities to attract investment, but no guarantees that the investment will contribute to increasing local productivity and development.

This serves to highlight the fact that SSA governments should remain aware that FDI can be transient in nature, which is most likely if the investment is motivated by accessing trade preferences that may themselves be temporary. Investment motivated by securing access to resources is more long term, but governments must ensure they receive the right price.

As discussed earlier, aid from China and India is largely indistinguishable from investment so it could usefully be treated as a complement to FDI that can be directed at development needs. China and India do attach conditions to their aid, typically related to 'access to natural resources or the purchase of goods and services provided by firms in the country providing support' (UNCTAD, 2010: 62). In this sense Chinese aid is quite similar to much of the FDI: the recipient gets something (the project is completed) but little extra. This restricts the benefits because it limits the potential linkages – an issue that recipients should address. On the other hand, the projects are concentrated in infrastructure and production and often involve participation of private firms so there is potential to promote local private sector involvement. 'There are a number of potential benefits from Chinese aid: better targeting on important infrastructure projects with long maturity and long-term potential; less bureaucracy (meaning lower transaction costs); greater efficiency and potentially faster response' (OECD, 2010: 89). The policy issue is integrating aid and investment from China and India into a coherent development strategy that includes diversifying production and exports and reflects the regional SSA needs.

Challenges facing SSA

Chinese and Indian imports represent challenges to SSA producers in domestic markets and in third-country export markets where SSA competes with China and India. The latter has been considered above (and in general is unlikely to be a major concern, except perhaps to countries like South Africa) so here we focus on import competition. The products where China and India have the largest import shares are not generally sectors in which SSA countries have significant production capacity, so domestic producers are not severely affected. In these cases issues may arise as the treatment of other sources of imports, notably the EU, alters and we consider this in the context of Economic Partnership Agreements (EPAs).

However, there is some evidence that competition from imports has displaced domestic producers in certain sectors and countries: 'it has been reported in many African countries that the influx of cheap manufactured products, mostly from China, presents challenges for local manufacturing firms ... [and some] traditional products that had been manufactured in Africa for several centuries are now being almost exclusively produced in China' (UNCTAD, 2010: 41). Kaplinsky et al. (2006) report anecdotal evidence from firms of Chinese imports displacing domestic clothing and furniture manufactures in Ghana and South Africa and clothing and footwear in Nigeria and Zambia. In Ethiopia, Asian imports undercut domestic shoe manufacturers so that a little under a third closed, almost a third contracted activity and the average firm size halved (Egziabher, 2006). The evidence that exists relates mostly to clothing, footwear and furniture; as found above (Table 2.6) these are among the products with the highest import share for China in some countries so the potential problem is real. Garments are worth considering as they encompass both import competition in domestic markets and threats to third-country markets as well as involving foreign investment.

The clothing sector

Competition from China and India in domestic and regional markets can limit the potential for SSA countries to develop a viable garment export sector. It is important to distinguish three main stages in the production chain: (1) raw materials, such as cotton and wool (which some SSA countries export); (2) textiles made from the raw materials (which is concentrated in China and India, with few SSA countries producing textiles); and (3) garments made from the textiles. The SSA countries in which the sector is important tend to import textiles to produce and export garments. They compete with (lower cost) producers, including China and India, in garment exports but benefit from preferential access, to the EU and USA in particular. One apparent advantage is that China and India see a benefit in providing textile inputs to SSA garment producers that can then avail of preferential access to the EU and North American garment markets (van Dijk, 2009).

Historically the clothing and textile sector has been an important entry point for industrialisation in low-income economies because of the relatively low technology intensity required. The global market for clothing is large and dynamic, characterised by short lead-times, inter-seasonal and intra-seasonal variety and tight logistics (Gereffi and Memedovic, 2003). The global clothing trade is a standard example of a value chain, involving global buyers with market power (such as retailers in the major consuming markets), global intermediary sourcing firms and disparate producers (Gereffi, 1999; Gibbon, 2003) with large volumes of clothing produced and sourced from the lowest priced suppliers. Trade preferences gave SSA producers an attractive position despite (labour) cost disadvantages, which attracted FDI and promoted exports, but few managed to move up the global value chain (Mauritius has been successful in producing high-value niche products). As discussed above, the evidence that FDI in clothing is footloose suggests that SSA producers do not have a secure place in the supply chain.

The largest SSA beneficiaries of garment sector FDI (from China and elsewhere) are exporters of clothing (especially to the USA) such as Kenya, Lesotho, Madagascar, Mauritius, South Africa and Swaziland. However, growth in China's and India's exports has been accompanied by a substantial decline in world manufacturing prices (Kaplinsky *et al.*, 2006). This poses a serious threat of crowding out the small range of SSA exports in third-country markets. Meanwhile, partly as a result of falling unit prices, China's exports flourished – for example, increasing by 58 per cent in the USA (Kaplinsky *et al.*, 2006). It is evident that the growth of China's exports had a direct adverse impact on exports from some SSA countries. The massive fall in employment across affected sectors in SSA represented a major setback for poverty reduction in respect of the scale of job losses and impact on female employees (Kaplinsky *et al.*, 2006). The benefits of reduced prices of imported Chinese clothing do not offset the large negative impacts, and to the extent that they displace local producers in domestic markets they exacerbate the situation.

Relevance of EU–SSA trade relations

Almost all SSA countries are party, in one way or another, to EPAs with the EU (Morrissey, 2010), a core feature of which is the elimination of tariffs on most imports from the EU. For the average SSA country, EPAs are likely to increase imports from the EU by 6–8 per cent and total imports by about 2 per cent (Morrissey and Zgovu, 2010: 74). Thus, although much of the consumer gain (from lower prices as tariffs on imports from the EU are eliminated) arises from increased imports of goods already previously imported from the EU, the EU will take market share from other countries. Whether this displaces China or India will differ across countries according to their pattern of trade in products in which the EU is competitive. Morrissey and Zgovu (2010: 69) identify Madagascar, Sudan, Uganda and United Republic of Tanzania as countries that have relatively high import shares from the rest of the world (imports from China and India are significant in all four, see Table 2.5 above) that may be displaced by tariff-free imports from the EU.

The EU is likely to displace some imports in the three most important sectors for imports from China and India (electrical and mechanical machinery and vehicles) and also in articles of iron or steel (important for China) and pharmaceuticals and cereals (important for India). The extent to which this may happen can only be identified at a country level. For example, Milner *et al.* (2010a: 88) note that the likely effect of an EPA for Mauritius is to increase imports from the EU particularly in the textiles, machinery and consumer electronics sectors. As China and India are suppliers of significant imports to Mauritius in these sectors, they are likely to lose market share as tariffs on EU goods are eliminated.

It is probable that the effects of EPAs on import shares of China and India in SSA countries will elicit a response. For example, as China and India offer preferential access to LDCs they may seek reciprocal preferences. An alternative scenario (which may already be happening) is that imports from China (and India) are tied to aid or investment projects, hence exempted from tariffs and resilient to EPA effects. If SSA countries succumb to these pressures they must be aware of the associated tariff revenue loss.

It should be noted that EPAs may offer a benefit in terms of making SSA more attractive to FDI to access the EU market. Chinese and Indian FDI has already responded to opportunities to avail of trade preferences (e.g., AGOA). As access is constrained by rules of origin requirements, such 'preference-seeking' FDI must deliver relatively high levels of domestic value added, hence promoting linkages and diversification (see also Milner *et al.*, 2010: 42–44). Investment is a major determinant of economic growth, but SSA countries tend to have relatively low levels of investment, and the productivity of investment tends to be low; this is one of the reasons why their growth performance has been less than desired. Increasing the level and productivity of investment is essential to delivering increased and sustained growth. Foreign investors deliver particular benefits in expanding the level of investment, in transferring technology, management and human capital, and potentially in linking with domestic firms (through joint ventures or supply chains). In general, while investment measures may aim to target particular sectors, they need not discriminate between domestic and foreign sources. In other words, even where the aim is to attract foreign investment any incentives offered can and should be available to domestic investors.

Policy responses to China and India

A number of policy issues should be addressed to allow SSA countries to benefit from expanded economic relationships with China and India. Building on the preceding discussion these are outlined here and summarised as recommendations in the final section. The suggestions are not inherently new. UNCTAD (2010: 102–105) provides a set of broad-based recommendations for African countries engaging with South–South co-operation. The responses we identify are similar, but more specific to trade and investment (including aid) with China and India. The recommendations regarding export diversification are similar to issues that have often been raised as to how SSA can respond to the changing global trade environment, e.g., Milner *et al.* (2010: 46–50) in the context of the erosion of trade preferences. The central issue is deriving widespread gains from export opportunities while recognising the adjustment needs of increased import competition. A specific concern is that China and India are competitive suppliers of labour-intensive products, i.e., in some of the sectors in which SSA countries are trying to develop production capacity. However, to the extent that China (and India) invest in SSA countries to promote manufacturing for export and to link with domestic suppliers, they can stimulate higher quality production and offer opportunities for SSA producers to position themselves better in global value chains (Knorringa, 2009). The problem, as discussed throughout this report, is that to date there is little evidence to indicate this is actually happening.

At the core of the response of SSA countries to their relationship with China and India is the need to target investments and co-operation to diversify production and exports. As noted above, it is important that SSA 'does not replicate the current pattern of economic relations with the rest of the world, in which Africa exports commodities and imports manufactures. In this regard, it would be desirable if African countries and their developing country partners manage their growing and evolving relationships in a manner that supports and enhances technological progress, capital accumulation and structural transformation in the region' (UNCTAD, 2010: 4). The language of Chinese and Indian economic co-operation is consistent with these objectives, but it is up to each SSA country to devise the appropriate diversification strategy, which is most likely to be effective if grounded in existing capabilities in value-added processing. Individual countries need to identify what resources they possess for which it is economically feasible to add value by establishing processing industries that can become competitive. The objective has been clearly stated elsewhere:

> [T]he focus should not be on attracting Southern FDI per se, rather it should be on how to create linkages between FDI and the domestic economy and also how to direct it to sectors where it can boost productive capacity, catalyse domestic investment, create

employment, spur regional integration and enhance integration into the global economy. The use of targeted incentives to encourage foreign investors to source inputs locally is one way to promote linkages between Southern FDI and the domestic economy. The promotion of joint ventures between African and Southern firms could also facilitate the diffusion of knowledge to local entrepreneurs and contribute to structural transformation. Another means through which developing countries could promote investment and boost industrialization in Africa is through the creation of special economic zones (SEZs). These zones have played an important part in China's economic development and have also been used by Mauritius as a source of surplus to develop the rest of the economy. It is interesting that China has recently taken the lead in establishing SEZs in the region. (UNCTAD, 2010: 96)

In respect to existing exports (mineral resources) the principal issue is the terms on which access to resources are negotiated and export revenues are shared to derive more benefit, especially promoting linkages with local firms (as goods or services providers), generating local employment and providing revenue to invest in development. A cornerstone of any mineral resource strategy is how SSA governments engage with the foreign investors, whether countries or firms, seeking to access and export their mineral resources. This is a bargaining issue where too often SSA governments have not secured the best deal for their country. Typically, the foreign investors want the unprocessed resource at the lowest price whereas clearly the SSA country benefits most where it gets the highest price, especially if it can undertake some of the processing.

Diversifying production to benefit from trade opportunities (identifying new markets) and expanding non-mineral exports requires an economy-wide investment strategy to relax supply constraints. The investments can be sector-specific, either to support new value-added industries processing resources or relaxing constraints in existing export sectors (LDCs could focus on those products they can export to China and India under preferences). Investment is also needed in infrastructure at a country and regional level; in areas such as transport and power generation regional projects are as important as national ones. A strategy to use aid and investment must have promoting linkages and private sector development at the core. As the projects supported by China and India are concentrated in infrastructure and production (including agriculture), are often long-term in orientation and frequently involve participation of firms (private or state-owned), there is potential to integrate financial inflows with a development strategy based on diversifying production and exports.

A related issue is addressing the nature of relationships between individual (small) SSA countries and large partner countries, where for Europe and the USA now read China and India. The large countries have a consistent strategy with each individual partner, but the individual countries have no clear strategy for engagement. Furthermore, individual countries are weaker when operating alone. 'Africa has not articulated a coherent regional approach to harnessing and managing these partnerships for its benefit ... [Chinese and Indian] actual engagement as well as implementation of projects is at the country level with often no link between these projects and the regional priorities of Africa' (UNCTAD, 2010: 26). A more regional approach can also be relevant to investment. 'However, so far the emphasis has been on national rather than regional infrastructure. African countries should encourage Southern partners to extend the scope of their infrastructure finance to the regional level as an important channel to reduce transactions costs, link national markets and boost intra-African trade and investment' (ibid.: 77).

Greater co-ordination for a regional SSA approach to China and India is desirable and it is becoming more feasible. One effect of EPAs is to promote regional groupings to negotiate with the EU, even if this has not worked well in all parts of SSA. The same groups could begin to engage with other countries. African countries have shown that they can work together in trade negotiations in the WTO.

> Africa's cooperation with developing countries in multilateral trade negotiations has had a significant impact in three key areas. First, it has enabled developing countries to influence the agenda and pace of the Doha Round negotiations ... By forming alliances, developing countries have now been able to influence developed countries to abandon three of the Singapore issues – investment, competition policy and government procurement. Second, the formation of alliances between Africa and other developing countries has increased their level of participation in the negotiation process [and increased the] bargaining power of African countries. Third, as a result of increased cooperation with Africa, several developing countries have put in place schemes to provide preferential market access for products originating from LDCs, most of which are in Africa. Brazil, China and India are examples of developing country partners that have put in place such schemes. (UNCTAD, 2010: 46)

As SSA countries develop co-operation with China and India it is important that they remain aware of the broader context of globally declining trade preference margins and the associated need for export diversification. Measures that make SSA more attractive to foreign investment and incorporate FDI in domestic development strategies can support this (Morrissey, 2010a: 231):

- Reform of regulatory and administrative procedures that reduce the costs of doing business (e.g., reducing the number of forms and licences required to invest or to start a business) encourages investment.
- Investment incentives can be targeted at sectors with potential for export growth, such as agri-processing. This can be especially important for LDCs aiming to avail of preferences granted by China and India.
- Measures that promote regional integration increase the potential market size and facilitate co-operation between SSA countries. This can attract foreign investors, generate scale economies and support a more co-ordinated engagement of SSA with economic partners.

Regional integration measures associated with EPAs provide an opportunity for SSA countries to attract higher levels of more diversified FDI: larger markets, lower transactions costs associated with trade and investment, and generally a more favourable business environment are all conducive. Although EPAs are most likely to make SSA more attractive to EU investors, there will be opportunities that are attractive to China and India.

Concluding recommendations

Economic relations with China and India have important effects on SSA countries, directly and indirectly and primarily through trade and investment. Although the initial and largest benefits accrue to exporters of fuels, minerals and metals, there is future potential for benefits to agriculture exports of oilseeds and vegetable oils, fish and seafood. As per capita incomes rise in China and India one may also anticipate increased demand for fruits and vegetables. Thus, although to date the significant export benefits have been limited to resource-exporting countries, there are future opportunities for other SSA countries. These opportunities will be squandered if viable domestic export producers are not supported.

Although the major products imported from China and India are machinery and equipment, vehicles and pharmaceutical products that do not compete with local industries (except perhaps in South Africa), an increasing import share has been captured by Chinese consumer goods (electronics, clothing, shoes), and Indian goods may follow. From an import perspective, the issue is whether competition from cheap imports is preventing the growth of domestic producers. SSA countries may have to increase their efforts to support domestic production and employment, but this should be by focusing on sectors that use available resources. Value-added processing offers the most viable manufacturing opportunities, especially in agri-business. The traditional policy of tariff protection is not viable in the context of progressive reductions of tariffs. Tariffs against imports from the EU will be reduced as EPAs are implemented, and China and India may seek some reciprocity for the duty-free access it grants to the least developed African countries.

A number of policy recommendations follow from the discussion and, as the details are country-specific, they are summarised in general terms. SSA countries should:

Increase their share of export revenues. Mineral exporters should ensure that they receive a competitive market price or share of the resource rent so that appropriate revenue is generated for the country. The revenue from exports should be invested in promoting development; this may be achieved most effectively through a designated, transparent fund.

Target new markets. Producers of non-mineral (soft) commodities should be supported in identifying opportunities to export to China and India through the provision of market information and access to networks. This is especially relevant for LDCs, which are granted preferential access to China and India for most commodities, and has potential for a wide variety of agricultural commodities.

Base effective export diversification on identifying value-added activities to process available resources. Individual countries should identify the resources they possess and where there are feasible opportunities (e.g., adequate supply to reach an efficient scale of production, access to inputs such as energy) to establish processing industries.

Understand that tariff protection is not a good policy response. Imports from China and India can compete with some domestic producers, but governments should only support (by measures to increase productivity) local firms that can become competitive.

Develop a co-ordinated investment strategy. SSA governments should ensure that aid and investment projects by China and India contribute to the local economy and development. This requires that projects link to sectors governments want to develop or provide national and regional infrastructure to increase productive efficiency and reduce trade costs. Investment by China and India is (legitimately) motivated by their own commercial interests and cannot be assumed to assist the integration of SSA producers into global value chains. The experience with garments cautions that such investment can be transitory.

Co-operate with each other. More effective engagement with China and India is possible if SSA countries co-operate. A co-ordinated or at least consistent approach to terms of access to mineral resources would increase the bargaining power of SSA countries and allow a greater share of the revenue to remain in the source economy. Co-operation has strengthened Africa's position in trade negotiations, such as in the WTO, and would also encourage regional investment projects.

Develop policies that recognise the broader trade environment. Relations with China and India will be affected by trade agreements with other parties, notably EPAs with the EU but also future developments in the WTO. Whilst EPAs may allow the EU to capture some market share from China and India in SSA imports, as they enhance preferential access to the EU, they will also make SSA more attractive for investment.

These policy recommendations are not inherently specific to relations with China and India. African countries should strive to avoid the 'resource curse' by negotiating access to resources more transparently with all countries or multinationals, and should strive to use aid and investment from all sources more effectively. New economic partners provide new opportunities, but the underlying issues are unchanged and SSA should avoid the errors of the past. SSA countries should not look to China and India to provide support for the development of domestic production, although they should not neglect opportunities that arise. Foreign investment delivers the greatest benefits when it provides linkages to the local economy, such as through employment or demand for local supplies. Chinese investment has not evidently delivered these benefits, and this is an issue that governments should monitor.

Ultimately, African development is its own responsibility. This means that SSA governments should ensure that they receive and use strategically the revenue from export earnings, which is the major benefit of trade with China and India, and should strive to realise all opportunities to diversify production and exports.

Notes

1. It is not obvious why this is the case as the Congo is a small, low-income state not obviously distinct from Democratic Republic of the Congo, or other LDCs, in terms of income or fragility (Guillaumont, 2009: 15).

References

Ajakaiye, O (2006) 'China and Africa – Opportunities and Challenges', presentation at the African Union Task Force on the Strategic Partnership Between Africa and Emerging Countries of the South, Addis Ababa, Ethiopia, 11–13 September.

Besada, H (2008) 'The Implications of China's Ascendancy for Africa', *Working Paper 40*, The Centre for International Governance Innovation, Ontario, Canada.

Bosshard, P (2008) 'China's Environmental Footprint in Africa', *China in Africa Policy Briefing*, 3, South African Institute of International Affairs (SAIIA), April.

Chaponniere, J-R (2009) 'Chinese Aid to Africa: Origins, Forms and Issues', in van Dijk (ed), *The New Presence of China in Africa*, Amsterdam University Press for EADI, Amsterdam, pp. 55–82.

DFID (Department for International Development) (2005) 'The Effects of China and India's Growth and Trade Liberalisation on Poverty in Africa', *Final Report*, DCP 70, May, DFID, London.

Egziabher, T G (2006) 'Asian Imports and Coping Strategies of Medium, Small and Micro Firms: The Case of Footwear Sector in Ethiopia', *mimeo*, Addis Ababa University.

Finger, M (2008) 'Evolving Wave of Competition in the International Market: Challenges for Africa Through the Rise of China and India', *Working paper*, Economic Research and Statistics Division, World Trade Organization, Geneva.

Gereffi, G (1999) 'International Trade and Industrial Upgrading in the Apparel Commodity Chain', *Journal of International Economics*, 48(1), pp. 37–70.

Gereffi, G and Memedovic, O (2003) 'The Global Apparel Value Chain: What Prospects for Upgrading by Developing Countries?', *Sector Studies Series*, United Nations Industrial Development Organization (UNIDO), Vienna.

Gibbon, P (2003) 'The African Growth and Opportunity Act and the Global Commodity Chain for Clothing', *World Development*, 31(11), pp. 1809–1827.

Giovannetti, G and Sanfilippo, M (2009) 'Do Chinese Exports Crowd-out African Goods? An Econometric Analysis by Country and Sector', *European Journal of Development Research*, 21(4), pp. 506–530.

Gottschalk, R (2005) 'The Asian Drivers: Financial Flows Into and Out of Asia and Implications for Developing Countries', paper presented at the Asian Drivers Workshop, Institute of Development Studies, 9–10 May.

Gu, J (2009) 'China's Private Enterprises in Africa and the Implications for African Development', *European Journal of Development Research*, 21(4), pp. 570–587.

Guillaumont, P (2009) *Caught in a Trap: Identifying the Least Developed Countries*, Economica, Paris.

Kaplinsky, R (2007) 'The Impact of China and India on the SSA: A Methodological Framework', prepared for African Economic Research Consortium (AERC), Department of Policy and Practice, The Open University, March.

Kaplinsky, R, McCormick, D and Morris, M (2006) 'Dangling by a Thread: Can SSA Survive the Chinese Scissors?', paper prepared for Africa Policy Division, DFID, Institute of Development Studies, Brighton.

Kaplinsky, R and Morris, M (2008) 'Do the Asian Drivers Undermine Export-oriented Industrialization in SSA?', *World Development*, 36(2), pp. 254–273.

—— (2009) 'Chinese FDI in Sub-Saharan Africa: Engaging with Large Dragons', *European Journal of Development Research*, 21(4), pp. 551–569.

Kaplinsky, R and Santos Paulino, A (2006) 'A Disaggregated Analysis of EU Imports: Implications for the Study of Patterns of Trade and Technology', *Cambridge Journal of Economics*, 30(4), pp. 587–611.

Katti, V, Chahoud, T and Kaushik, A (2009) 'India's Development Cooperation – Opportunities and Challenges for International Development Cooperation', *Briefing Paper 3/2009*, German Development Institute (DIE), Bonn.

Knorringa, P (2009) 'Responsible Production in Africa: The Rise of China as a Threat or Opportunity', in van Dijk (ed), *The New Presence of China in Africa*, Amsterdam University Press for EADI, Amsterdam, pp. 177–198.

Kragelund, P and van Dijk, M (2009) 'China's Investment in Africa', in van Dijk (ed), *The New Presence of China in Africa*, Amsterdam University Press for EADI, Amsterdam, pp. 83–100.

Lancaster, C (2007) The Chinese Aid System, *CGD Essay June 2007*, Centre for Global Development, Washington, DC.

Mayer, J and Fajarnes, P (2008) 'Tripling Africa's Primary Exports: What, How, Where?', *Journal of Development Studies*, 44(1), pp. 80–102.

Milner, C, Morrissey, O and Rudaheranwa, N (2000) 'Policy and Non-policy Barriers to Trade and Implicit Taxation of Exports in Uganda', *Journal of Development Studies*, 37(2), pp. 67–90.

Milner, C, Morrissey, O and Zgovu, E (2010) *Policy Responses to Trade Preference Erosion: Options for Developing Countries*, Commonwealth Secretariat, London.

—— (2010a) 'Adjusting to an EPA: Evidence for Mauritius', chapter 4 in Morrissey (ed), *Assessing Prospective Trade Policy: Methods Applied to EU-ACP Economic Partnership Agreements*, Routledge, London, pp. 83–104.

Minson, A (2008) 'China's Preferential Trade Policy in Africa', *China in Africa Policy Briefing*, 1, South African Institute of International Affairs (SAIIA), February.

Morrissey, O (2005) 'Imports and Implementation: Neglected Aspects of Trade in the Report of the Commission for Africa', *Journal of Development Studies*, 41(4), pp. 1133–1153.

—— (2010) (ed) *Assessing Prospective Trade Policy: Methods Applied to EU-ACP Economic Partnership Agreements*, Routledge, London.

—— (2010a) 'Conclusions: EPAs to Promote ACP Development', chapter 10 in Morrissey (ed), pp. 223–234.

Morrissey, O and Zgovu, E (2010) 'The Impact of EPAs on ACP Imports and Welfare', chapter 3 in Morrissey (ed), pp. 60–82.

OECD (Organisation for Economic Co-operation and Development (2010), *Perspectives on Global Development 2010: Shifting Wealth*, OECD Development Centre, Paris.

Oyejide, T A, Bankole, A S and Adewuyi, A O (2009) 'China-Africa Trade Relations: Insights from AERC Scoping Studies', *European Journal of Development Research*, 21(4), pp. 485–505.

Rumbaugh, T and Blancher, N (2004) 'China: International Trade and WTO Accession', *IMF Working Paper 04/36*, International Monetary Fund, Washington, DC.

Taylor, I (2010) *China's New Role in Africa*, Lynne Rienner Publishers, Boulder, CO.

UNCTAD (United Nations Conference on Trade and Development) (2003) *World Investment Report 2003*, UNCTAD, Geneva.

—— (2004) 'India's Outward FDI: A Giant Awakening', UNCTAD/DITE/IIAB/2004/1, UNCTAD, Geneva.

—— (2008) *Trade and Development Report 2008*, UNCTAD, Geneva.

—— (2009) *World Investment Report 2009*, UNCTAD, Geneva.

—— (2010) *Economic Development in Africa Report 2010: South-South Cooperation – Africa and the New Forms of Development Partnership*, UNCTAD, Geneva.

van Dijk, M P (2009) (ed), *The New Presence of China in Africa*, Amsterdam University Press for EADI, Amsterdam.

WTO (World Trade Organization) (2001) *International Trade Statistics 2001*, WTO, Geneva.

—— (2009) *International Trade Statistics 2009*, WTO, Geneva.

—— (2010) *Trade Policy Review China April 2010*, WTO, Geneva.

Appendix Tables

Table A1. HS two-digit product code and descriptions

HS2	Description
01	Live animals
02	Meat and edible meat offal
03	Fish, seafood
04	Dairy produce, birds' eggs, honey
05	Other products of animal origin
06	Live trees, plants, bulbs, roots, cut flowers
07	Edible vegetables, certain roots and tubers
08	Edible fruit and nuts, citrus or melon
09	Coffee, tea, mate and spices
10	Cereals
11	Milling products, malt, starch, gluten
12	Oil seeds, seeds, straw, fodder
13	Lac, gums, resins, etc.
14	Other vegetable products
15	Animal or vegetable fats & oils
16	Edible preparations of meat, seafood
17	Sugars and sugar confectionery
18	Cocoa and cocoa preparations
19	Prep. of cereals, flour, starch or milk
20	Preparations of vegetables, fruits, nuts
21	Miscellaneous edible preparations
22	Beverages, spirits and vinegar
23	Food residues & waste; animal feed
24	Tobacco and manufactured substitutes
25	Salt, sulphur, earth & stone, plaster
26	Ores, slag and ash
27	Mineral fuels, oils

Table A1. (continued)

HS2	Description
28	Inorganic chemicals
29	Organic chemicals
30	Pharmaceutical products
31	Fertilisers
32	Dyes, paint & varnish; extracts
33	Essential oils; perfumery, cosmetic
34	Soap; waxes; polish; candles
35	Modified starch; glues; enzymes
36	Explosives; combustible preparations
37	Photographic or cinematographic goods
38	Miscellaneous chemical products
39	Plastics and articles thereof
40	Rubber and articles thereof
41	Raw hides, skins and leather
42	Leather articles
43	Fur skins and artificial, manufactures
44	Wood and articles of wood; charcoal
45	Cork and articles of cork
46	Manufactures of straw,
47	Pulp of wood, etc.
48	Paper & paperboard
49	Printed books, etc.
50	Silk, including yarns and woven fabric
51	Wool & animal hair, yarn & woven fabric
52	Cotton, yarn and woven fabric
53	Other vegetable textile fibres
54	Manmade filaments, yarns & woven fabrics
55	Manmade staple fibres, yarns & woven fabrics
56	Wadding; yarns; twine, ropes, cables
57	Carpets and textile floor coverings
58	Special woven fabrics
59	Treated fabrics; industrial textiles
60	Knitted or crocheted fabrics
61	Apparel, knitted or crocheted
62	Apparel, not knitted or crocheted

Table A1. (continued)

HS2	Description
63	Worn clothing etc.
64	Footwear
65	Headgear and parts
66	Umbrellas, walking-sticks, etc.
67	Prepared feathers, artificial flowers; human hair
68	Articles of stone, plaster, cement, etc.
69	Ceramic products
70	Glass and glassware
71	Natural or cultured pearls, precious stones
72	Iron and steel
73	Articles of iron or steel
74	Copper and articles thereof
75	Nickel and articles thereof
76	Aluminium and articles thereof
78	Lead and articles thereof
79	Zinc and articles thereof
80	Tin and articles thereof
81	Other base metals; articles thereof
82	Tools, implements, cutlery, of base metal
83	Miscellaneous articles of base metal
84	Nuclear, machinery & mechanical
85	Electric machinery; electronic equipment
86	Railway; locomotives, rolling stock
87	Vehicles (not railway); parts
88	Aircraft, etc.
89	Ships, etc.
90	Optical, precision, surgical etc.
91	Clocks and watches and parts
92	Musical instruments; parts
93	Arms and ammunition
94	Furniture and furnishings
95	Toys, games & sports equipment; parts
96	Miscellaneous manufactured articles
97	Works of art, antiques
99	Imports by privileged persons, etc.

Table A2. Major SSA exporters to China and India (US$ millions)

China	2000	2003	2005	2008	2009
All SSA	**5,336.30**	**7,881.11**	**19,219.01**	**50,502.27**	**37,120.44**
Angola	1,842.69	2,205.94	6,581.83	22,382.52	14,675.83
Congo	323.72	814.66	2,278.03	3,731.70	1,738.81
Dem. Rep. of Congo	0.98	26.24	175.77	1,583.86	1,136.45
Equatorial Guinea	319.48	411.89	1,437.83	2,267.87	1,055.07
Nigeria	307. 30	71.66	526.88	508.38	896.53
South Africa	1,037.29	1,839.99	3,443.05	9,234.97	8,693.25
Sudan	731.73	1,441.82	2,614.46	6,325.89	4,684.82
Zambia	69.39	47.88	252.06	522.50	1,272.46

India	2000	2003	2005	2007	2008
All SSA	**2,742.83**	**2,808.76**	**4,084.35**	**13,602.30**	**20,885.15**
Angola			2.83	920.24	1,289.28
Congo	8.80	4.29	40.90	84.92	500.11
Dem. Rep. of Congo	0.28	0.10	5.17	17.12	114.32
Equatorial Guinea		0.17	0.02	72.73	83.31
Nigeria	757.45	86.98	62.36	7,017.40	10,124.67
South Africa	1,394.91	1,945.74	2,683.48	3,181.70	5,551.21
Sudan	7.36	30.30	27.67	242.51	545.76
Zambia	13.41	19.24	34.87	71.83	139.31

Source: Authors analysis using data from World Integrated Trade Solution (WITS)
http://wits.worldbank.org/wits/

Table A3. SSA imports by value (US$ millions) and origin, 2003

	Value (US$ millions)	SSA (%)	China (%)	India (%)	Rest of world (%)
All SSA	**95,564.9**	**17.5**	**5.7**	**1.3**	**75.5**
Benin	892.0	27.0	7.1	1.7	64.3
Botswana	3,964.0	86.2	0.6	0.2	13.0
Burkina Faso	785.9	45.3	2.7	2.3	49.7
Burundi	144.7	47.2	0.9	0.0	51.9
Cameroon	2,163.4	14.7	4.0	1.5	79.8
Cape Verde	354.8	5.7	1.1	0.0	93.1
Central African Rep.	99.6	14.2	2.5	0.0	83.4
Comoros	45.9	17.9	1.0	0.9	80.3
Côte d'Ivoire	3,535.9	18.4	3.5	0.0	78.1
Ethiopia	2,685.9	1.9	11.7	0.0	86.4
Gabon	770.0	6.6	1.1	0.0	92.3
Gambia	162.6	9.2	5.1	0.0	85.7
Ghana	3,210.2	24.5	5.6	0.0	69.9
Guinea-Bissau	63.9	14.7	19.2	0.0	66.0
Kenya	3,475.0	11.6	2.5	0.0	85.9
Lesotho	1,115.0	82.3	2.6	0.5	14.6
Madagascar	1,318.1	12.4	14.8	4.0	68.9
Malawi	785.4	59.3	2.8	4.8	33.1
Mali	1,271.1	40.9	3.1	2.9	53.1
Mauritius	2,389.5	16.2	8.4	0.0	75.4
Mozambique	1,753.0	36.0	2.3	3.9	57.8
Namibia	1,427.9	81.3	1.3	0.0	17.4
Niger	565.6	34.7	9.4	3.2	52.7
Nigeria	14,892.5	4.8	7.2	0.0	88.0
Rwanda	261.2	48.4	1.9	0.0	49.7
São Tomé	40.8	3.8	0.1	0.0	96.1
Senegal	2,398.2	18.7	2.7	2.2	76.4
Seychelles	412.7	16.6	0.8	2.2	80.4
South Africa	34,543.1	3.1	6.4	1.2	89.3
Sudan	2,897.9	3.7	10.7	5.0	80.6
Swaziland	1,457.5	85.6	1.5	0.0	12.9
Togo	568.4	18.6	4.1	1.4	75.9
Uganda	1,375.1	35.2	5.1	7.4	52.3
United Rep. of Tanzania	2,164.3	19.9	5.4	7.8	66.9
Zambia	1,573.8	67.5	2.7	1.6	28.1

Source: Authors analysis using data from WITS

Table A4. SSA imports by value (US$ millions) and origin, 2005

	Value (US$ millions)	SSA (%)	China (%)	India (%)	Rest of world (%)
All SSA	**125,531.0**	**18.3**	**7.7**	**2.8**	**71.2**
Benin	898.7	26.3	8.8	1.6	63.3
Botswana	3,162.3	86.7	1.1	0.7	11.5
Burkina Faso	1,160.7	45.5	2.7	2.7	49.1
Burundi	258.2	28.3	4.2	4.1	63.4
Cameroon	2,735.2	26.5	5.2	1.3	67.0
Cape Verde	438.2	3.1	1.4	0.0	95.4
Central African Rep.	186.3	28.2	1.8	0.0	70.0
Comoros	85.2	24.2	1.6	3.6	70.6
Côte d'Ivoire	5,865.0	27.3	3.1	1.4	68.3
Ethiopia	4,094.8	3.2	12.6	6.0	78.2
Gabon	1,471.9	8.5	1.8	0.8	88.8
Gambia	259.6	16.1	9.3	4.7	69.9
Ghana	4,878.4	19.6	8.1	3.4	69.0
Guinea	1,647.8	18.2	3.9	2.3	75.6
Guinea-Bissau	111.7	42.9	2.4	0.0	54.6
Kenya	5,846.2	12.7	5.2	5.6	76.5
Madagascar	1,685.9	15.6	13.9	5.9	64.5
Malawi	1,165.2	63.7	2.9	4.7	28.8
Mali	1,543.6	48.2	4.9	2.4	44.5
Mauritius	3,160.1	11.2	9.8	6.9	72.1
Mozambique	2,408.2	44.9	2.8	4.0	48.2
Namibia	2,515.8	84.5	1.6	0.5	13.4
Niger	735.6	32.8	5.5	3.9	57.9
Rwanda	415.0	42.4	3.0	3.6	50.9
São Tomé	49.9	1.2	0.2	0.0	98.6
Senegal	3,497.5	17.6	3.6	3.3	75.5
Seychelles	674.9	9.4	1.0	2.0	87.6
South Africa	55,032.6	3.9	9.0	2.0	85.1
Sudan	7,366.8	2.1	17.9	4.3	75.7
Swaziland	1,656.1	86.6	4.0	0.0	9.4
Togo	592.6	16.3	13.2	2.4	68.2
Uganda	2,054.1	35.4	5.3	6.4	52.8
United Rep. of Tanzania	3,246.8	19.4	6.9	5.9	67.8
Zambia	2,558.0	58.3	3.3	2.3	36.0
Zimbabwe	2,072.3	76.3	2.4	1.7	19.6

Source: Authors analysis using data from WITS

Table A5. SSA imports by value (US$ millions) and origin, 2008

	Value (US$ millions)	SSA (%)	China (%)	India (%)	Rest of world (%)
All SSA	**219,601.7**	**14.1**	**10.7**	**4.2**	**71.0**
Botswana	5,098.7	80.4	2.8	0.7	16.1
Burundi	315.2	29.7	7.3	5.0	57.9
Cape Verde	824.2	1.9	1.7	0.0	96.4
Côte d'Ivoire	7,883.7	33.0	6.9	1.7	58.4
Ethiopia	8,680.3	3.2	20.2	7.3	69.3
Gambia	329.4	14.2	10.8	1.7	73.3
Ghana	9,057.7	19.7	11.7	4.3	64.3
Guinea	1,907.9	8.0	6.7	2.6	82.7
Kenya	11,127.8	9.5	8.4	11.8	70.3
Madagascar	3,845.9	9.6	21.0	4.7	64.7
Malawi	2,203.7	60.8	3.3	4.8	31.1
Mali	3,338.9	38.0	10.2	2.0	49.8
Mauritius	4,669.7	11.3	11.5	23.9	53.2
Mozambique	4,007.8	31.6	3.9	3.6	60.9
Namibia	4,688.6	69.7	3.3	3.5	23.6
Niger	1,247.5	19.8	12.6	2.3	65.3
Nigeria	28,193.6	6.0	15.2	3.6	75.1
Rwanda	1,145.6	44.4	8.4	3.5	43.8
Senegal	6,527.6	18.5	6.0	2.1	73.4
Seychelles	911.9	11.3	2.0	2.9	83.9
South Africa	87,593.1	5.2	11.3	2.6	80.9
Sudan	16,416.7	3.3	7.9	3.5	85.3
Uganda	4,525.9	20.5	8.1	10.4	61.0
Zambia	5,060.5	60.6	4.5	3.8	31.2

Source: Authors analysis using data from WITS.

Table A6. Chinese imports at HS2 level (US$ '000), 2008

HS2	Total value	RSA (%)	Other SSA (%)	All SSA (%)	Rest of world (%)
Total	**1,132,562,161.4**	**0.8**	**3.6**	**4.5**	**95.5**
01	104,292.1	2.8	0.1	2.9	97.1
02	2,319,967.5	0.0	0.0	0.0	100.0
03	3,648,212.3	0.1	0.3	0.4	99.6
04	872,777.6	0.0	0.0	0.0	100.0
05	255,232.1	0.1	1.2	1.3	98.7
06	90,896.0	0.2	0.1	0.3	99.7
07	584,197.7	0.0	0.0	0.0	100.0
08	1,237,695.2	0.4	0.3	0.7	99.3
09	101,158.2	0.6	4.7	5.3	94.7
10	698,520.3	0.0	0.2	0.2	99.8
11	233,932.3	0.0	0.0	0.0	100.0
12	23,182,452.8	0.0	0.5	0.5	99.5
13	110,459.5	0.0	2.8	2.8	97.2
14	78,582.5	0.0	0.7	0.7	99.3
15	11,244,843.4	0.4	0.0	0.4	99.6
16	79,465.5	0.0	0.4	0.4	99.6
17	424,063.8	0.0	0.0	0.0	100.0
18	312,958.5	0.0	36.2	36.2	63.8
19	718,541.2	0.0	0.0	0.0	100.0
20	300,710.6	2.7	0.0	2.7	97.3
21	466,361.9	0.0	0.1	0.1	99.9
22	1,137,278.8	0.5	0.0	0.5	99.5
23	1,864,002.7	0.7	0.4	1.1	98.9
24	787,784.5	0.4	19.0	19.4	80.6
25	6,116,497.8	0.4	0.1	0.5	99.5
26	85,936,802.7	4.7	2.9	7.6	92.4
27	169,251,777.1	0.1	21.0	21.0	79.0
28	9,191,586.4	0.1	1.3	1.4	98.6
29	39,179,145.7	0.1	0.0	0.1	99.9
30	4,902,402.8	0.0	0.0	0.0	100.0
31	3,481,222.2	0.0	0.0	0.0	100.0
32	4,023,463.3	0.3	0.0	0.3	99.7
33	1,115,500.3	0.0	0.1	0.1	99.9
34	2,199,780.4	0.1	0.0	0.1	99.9

Table A6. (continued)

HS2	Total value	RSA (%)	Other SSA (%)	All SSA (%)	Rest of world (%)
35	1,543,507.1	0.0	0.0	0.0	100.0
36	33,188.1	0.0	0.0	0.0	100.0
37	1,513,870.7	0.0	0.0	0.0	100.0
38	9,278,746.5	0.2	0.0	0.2	99.8
39	48,906,070.9	0.2	0.1	0.2	99.8
40	11,902,861.3	0.0	0.0	0.1	99.9
41	5,639,531.1	0.9	1.0	1.9	98.1
42	700,845.9	0.0	0.0	0.0	100.0
43	454,911.9	0.0	0.0	0.0	100.0
44	8,023,379.1	0.0	12.3	12.3	87.7
45	35,357.5	0.0	0.0	0.0	100.0
46	7,582.8	0.0	0.5	0.5	99.5
47	12,260,271.9	0.3	0.1	0.4	99.6%
48	4,363,341.3	0.2	0.0	0.2	99.8
49	821,362.9	0.0	0.0	0.0	100.0
50	116,648.7	0.0	0.0	0.0	100.0
51	2,620,072.9	3.1	0.0	3.1	96.9
52	7,444,854.2	0.0	3.9	4.0	96.0
53	412,572.8	0.0	3.0	3.0	97.0
54	3,651,304.2	0.0	0.0	0.0	100.0
55	2,520,297.7	0.0	0.0	0.0	100.0
56	998,570.1	0.0	0.0	0.0	100.0
57	101,289.7	0.1	0.0	0.1	99.9
58	737,712.5	0.0	0.0	0.0	100.0
59	1,727,834.9	0.0	0.0	0.0	100.0
60	2,311,296.2	0.0	0.0	0.0	100.0
61	853,703.7	0.0	0.1	0.1	99.9
62	1,221,965.6	0.0	0.2	0.2	99.8
63	279,822.0	0.1	0.0	0.1	99.9
64	1,015,343.7	0.0	0.0	0.0	100.0
65	24,355.6	0.1	0.0	0.1	99.9
66	6,435.7	0.0	0.0	0.0	100.0
67	192,942.6	0.0	0.2	0.3	99.7
68	882,743.7	0.1	0.0	0.1	99.9
69	446,977.8	0.0	0.0	0.0	100.0

Table A6. (continued)

HS2	Total value	RSA (%)	Other SSA (%)	All SSA (%)	Rest of world (%)
70	3,420,010.9	0.0	0.0	0.0	100.0
71	7,547,712.7	22.6	0.9	23.5	76.5
72	24,533,997.6	3.7	0.0	3.7	96.3
73	10,547,822.8	0.1	0.0	0.1	99.9
74	26,051,360.5	0.6	3.3	3.9	96.1
75	5,061,910.5	2.0	0.0	2.0	98.0
76	6,834,934.8	1.1	0.2	1.3	98.7
78	126,691.8	0.0	0.1	0.1	99.9
79	897,284.9	0.0	3.5	3.5	96.5
80	468,872.0	0.0	0.0	0.0	100.0
81	1,317,057.3	0.9	29.1	29.9	70.1
82	2,330,553.6	0.0	0.0	0.0	100.0
83	1,345,439.9	0.0	0.0	0.0	100.0
84	140,008,570.3	0.0	0.0	0.0	100.0
85	265,262,894.9	0.0	0.0	0.0	100.0
86	1,447,099.0	0.0	0.0	0.0	100.0
87	26,962,790.4	0.0	0.0	0.0	100.0
88	10,055,770.8	0.0	0.0	0.0	100.0
89	1,288,066.7	0.0	0.0	0.0	100.0
90	77,708,548.2	0.0	0.0	0.0	100.0
91	1,859,544.3	0.0	0.0	0.0	100.0
92	197,221.0	0.0	0.1	0.1	99.9
93	2,987.0	0.0	0.0	0.0	100.0
94	1,526,474.7	0.1	0.0	0.1	99.9
95	1,193,099.9	0.0	0.0	0.0	100.0
96	831,605.5	0.0	0.0	0.0	100.0
97	22,071.8	0.8	0.8	1.6	98.4
99	4,407,628.8	35.2	0.0	35.2	64.8

Note: RSA refers to the Republic of South Africa.

Source: Authors analysis using data from WITS

Table A7. Indian imports at HS2 level (US$ '000), 2008

	Value (US$ '000)	RSA (%)	Other SSA (%)	All SSA (%)	Rest of world (%)
Total	315,712,105.6	1.8	4.9	6.6	93.4
01	8,507.4	0.0	0.0	0.0	100.0
02	742.3	0.0	0.0	0.0	100.0
03	57,095.1	0.0	0.0	0.0	100.0
04	18,189.3	0.0	0.0	0.0	100.0
05	14,190.3	0.0	2.1	2.2	97.8
06	12,035.8	1.1	0.9	2.0	98.0
07	1,464,725.1	0.0	5.6	5.6	94.4
08	1,171,243.5	0.2	49.0	49.2	50.8
09	277,493.8	0.0	14.8	14.8	85.2
10	274,790.5	0.0	0.0	0.0	100.0
11	21,184.6	0.0	0.0	0.0	100.0
12	155,144.3	0.6	28.4	29.0	71.0
13	84,989.3	0.0	12.0	12.0	88.0
14	5,054.3	0.0	0.0	0.0	100.0
15	3,513,578.0	0.0	0.0	0.0	100.0
16	3,533.3	0.0	0.8	0.8	99.2
17	69,651.7	0.0	0.0	0.0	100.0
18	58,263.5	0.1	35.7	35.8	64.2
19	34,674.6	0.0	0.0	0.0	100.0
20	40,021.3	1.0	0.0	1.0	99.0
21	56,346.0	0.3	0.1	0.4	99.6
22	212,278.1	0.6	0.0	0.7	99.3
23	128,662.5	0.7	0.0	0.8	99.2
24	17,296.2	0.0	17.4	17.4	82.6
25	2,537,999.5	0.2	3.2	3.4	96.6
26	5,250,223.2	6.3	8.3	14.5	85.5
27	115,880,437.5	0.8	11.1	11.9	88.1
28	4,881,060.5	13.6	4.1	17.7	82.3
29	8,869,770.7	0.7	0.0	0.8	99.2
30	901,273.9	2.9	0.0	2.9	97.1
31	12,283,853.0	0.2	0.0	0.2	99.8
32	870,214.9	1.1	0.7	1.8	98.2
33	283,399.7	0.1	1.0	1.0	99.0
34	319,266.0	0.0	0.0	0.0	100.0

Table A7. (continued)

	Value (US$ '000)	RSA (%)	Other SSA (%)	All SSA (%)	Rest of world (%)
35	150,382.1	0.3	0.0	0.3	99.7%
36	7,593.5	0.0	0.0	0.0	100.0
37	306,041.5	0.0	0.0	0.0	100.0
38	1,978,668.2	0.3	0.0	0.4	99.6
39	4,468,323.5	0.1	0.1	0.3	99.7
40	1,815,150.4	0.3	0.0	0.3%	99.7
41	484,938.4	0.1	4.9	5.1	94.9
42	98,398.2	0.0	0.0	0.0	100.0
43	2,798.3	0.0	0.1	0.1	99.9
44	1,478,846.3	0.0	17.7	17.7	82.3
45	4,254.8	0.0	0.0	0.0	100.0
46	1,112.8	0.0	0.0	0.0	100.0
47	865,661.3	5.1	0.1	5.3	94.7
48	1,847,388.5	0.1	0.0	0.1	99.9
49	525,300.4	0.0	0.0	0.1	99.9
50	370,874.7	0.0	0.0	0.0	100.0
51	320,600.7	6.1	0.5	6.6	93.4
52	710,955.3	0.1	16.7	16.9	83.1
53	87,359.6	0.0	1.3	1.3	98.7
54	533,276.6	0.8	0.1	0.8	99.2
55	286,281.6	0.0	0.0	0.0	100.0
56	104,098.6	0.0	0.1	0.1	99.9
57	55,092.8	0.9	0.2	1.0	99.0
58	95,974.4	0.0	0.0	0.0	100.0
59	539,521.2	0.0	0.0	0.0	100.0
60	144,856.8	0.0	0.0	0.0	100.0
61	49,971.4	0.0	0.0	0.0	100.0
62	87,407.9	0.1	0.6	0.6	99.4
63	182,947.3	0.0	0.0	0.0	100.0
64	172,277.3	0.0	0.0	0.0	100.0
65	3,860.8	0.5	0.0	0.5	99.5
66	18,121.7	0.0	0.0	0.0	100.0
67	10,936.4	0.0	0.2	0.3	99.7
68	308,400.0	0.1	0.0	0.1	99.9
69	523,868.1	0.1	0.0	0.1	99.9

Table A7. (continued)

	Value (US$ '000)	RSA (%)	Other SSA (%)	All SSA (%)	Rest of world (%)
70	467,913.4	0.1	0.0	0.1	99.9
71	35,093,293.5	8.1	0.2	8.3	91.7
72	10,772,430.5	2.4	2.6	5.1	94.9
73	3,671,092.4	0.1	0.0	0.1	99.9
74	1,458,126.8	0.4	4.4	4.8	95.2
75	558,440.6	2.7	0.1	2.8	97.2
76	1,590,316.7	9.3	1.8	11.2	88.8
78	445,563.8	0.6	6.8	7.4	92.6
79	208,306.3	0.4	1.1	1.5	98.5
80	113,206.9	0.1	0.0	0.1	99.9
81	231,023.4	0.6	1.0	1.6	98.4
82	563,514.6	0.1	0.1	0.2	99.8
83	319,399.9	0.1	0.0	0.1	99.9
84	27,890,083.3	0.1	0.1	0.2	99.8
85	16,097,604.8	0.2	0.0	0.2	99.8
86	253,962.5	0.1	0.0	0.1	99.9
87	3,184,553.9	0.1	0.2	0.3	99.7
88	12,172,053.8	0.0	0.0	0.0	100.0
89	4,808,466.2	0.0	0.8	0.8	99.2
90	4,648,190.4	0.0	0.1	0.1%	99.9
91	149,194.1	0.0	0.1	0.1	99.9
92	17,353.3	0.0	0.0	0.0	100.0
93	15,820.7	41.0	0.1	41.1	58.9
94	639,303.4	0.0	0.0	0.1	99.9
95	156,542.3	0.0	0.0	0.0	100.0%
96	234,275.1	0.0	0.0	0.1	99.9
97	28,282.1	0.0	0.0	0.0	100.0
99	11,505,059.8	0.1	0.0	0.1	99.9

Note: RSA refers to the Republic of South Africa.

Source: Authors analysis using data from WITS

Table A8. Top four SSA HS2 imports from China and India, 2008

Country		China (US$ millions)	HS2 Codes and share (%)				India (US$ millions)	HS2 Codes and share (%)			
	Rank		1	2	3	4		1	2	3	4
Botswana	HS		84	71	85	73		30	84	85	73
	%	144.9	15	12	11	10	36.0	24	13	11	9
Burundi	HS		84	85	40	94		30	87	40	84
	%	23.2	25	9	9	8	15.9	43	12	6	4
Cape Verde	HS		84	85	94	69		84	30	85	87
	%	13.8	14	10	9	7	0.2	68	20	6	5
Côte d'Ivoire	HS		85	73	84	72		30	39	02	87
	%	542.1	22	11	10	6	131.5	16	9	9	8
Ethiopia	HS		85	84	87	73		72	85	30	84
	%	1,750.4	41	14	7	6	635.6	16	11	11	10
The Gambia	HS		52	85	34	15		10	30	52	76
	%	35.5	16	10	7	7	5.7	15	13	12	11
Ghana	HS		84	85	73	72		87	85	30	84
	%	1,060.7	15	15	9	8	392.5	17	12	10	9
Guinea	HS		85	87	84	73		87	10	30	85
	%	128.2	18	8	7	6	50.3	27	22	14	5
Kenya	HS		85	84	87	72		27	84	30	85
	%	932.2	17	17	10	5	1,309.5	38	12	9	8
Madagascar	HS		84	73	85	51		27	10	72	30
	%	808.7	23	17	11	9	180.8	40	12	10	8
Malawi	HS		85	84	31	64		30	87	84	72
	%	72.4	17	15	12	6	106.8	25	12	11	9
Mali	HS		85	84	87	72		72	30	10	84
	%	342.1	18	11	10	6	66.1	27	21	19	13
Mauritius	HS		85	84	52	73		27	52	30	10
	%	538.6	17	12	10	4	1,116.6	75	7	2	2
Mozambique	HS		87	84	85	73		87	30	85	84
	%	156.1	14	14	12	8	144.4	22	22	10	8
Namibia	HS		87	85	94	25		28	30	76	73
	%	153.3	17	16	11	10	162.4	42	15	12	11
Niger	HS		84	85	73	87		27	10	72	30
	%	156.8	40	9	7	5	29.0	35	25	11	11

Table A8. (continued)

Country		China (US$ millions)	China HS2 Codes and share (%)				India (US$ millions)	India HS2 Codes and share (%)			
	Rank		1	2	3	4		1	2	3	4
Nigeria	HS		84	85	87	69		84	87	85	30
	%	4,292.3	19	17	17	5	1,024.0	25	8	8	7
Rwanda	HS		85	73	84	82		30	72	87	84
	%	95.9	44	10	6	4	39.7	27	23	10	10
Senegal	HS		85	72	84	87		84	10	87	27
	%	390.2	15	12	11	5	139.8	16	12	9	9
Seychelles	HS		84	10	44	94		10	72	87	07
	%	17.8	11	8	7	7	26.3	30	9	6	6
South Africa	HS		85	84	64	87		27	85	30	87
	%	9,909.3	23	22	4	4	2,261.9	32	9	7	7
Sudan	HS		85	84	72	62		72	87	85	30
	%	1,295.6	27	18	13	6	579.4	69	8	5	3
Uganda	HS		85	84	64	87		27	30	72	87
	%	365.8	19	12	9	6	470.5	19	13	11	10
Zambia	HS		84	85	73	87		30	84	87	85
	%	227.2	30	16	15	6	191.6	42	26	6	4

Notes: HS2 sectors in **bold** are in 'top four' for both China and India.

Source: Authors analysis using data from WITS.

Table A9. Merchandise exports by region and selected economy

	1948	1953	1963	1973	1983	1993	2003	2008
World (US$ billions)	59	84	157	579	1,838	3,676	7,377	15,717
				Share (%)				
World %	100.0	100.0	100.0	100.0	100.0	100.0	100.0	100.0
United States	21.7	18.8	14.9	12.3	11.2	12.6	9.8	8.2
Canada	5.5	5.2	4.3	4.6	4.2	4.0	3.7	2.9
EU[a]	–	–	27.5	38.6	31.3	37.4	42.4	37.5
Germany[b]	1.4	5.3	9.3	11.6	9.2	10.3	10.2	9.3
France	3.4	4.8	5.2	6.3	5.2	6.0	5.3	3.9
Italy	11.3	9.0	7.8	5.1	4.0	4.6	4.1	3.4
United Kingdom	1.8	1.8	3.2	3.8	5.0	4.9	4.1	2.9
Africa	7.3	6.5	5.7	4.8	4.5	2.5	2.4	3.5
South Africa[c]	2.0	1.6	1.5	1.0	1.0	0.7	0.5	0.5
Asia	14.0	13.4	12.5	14.9	19.1	26.1	26.2	27.7
China	0.9	1.2	1.3	1.0	1.2	2.5	5.9	9.1
Japan	0.4	1.5	3.5	6.4	8.0	9.9	6.4	5.0
India	2.2	1.3	1.0	0.5	0.5	0.6	0.8	1.1
Six East Asian traders[d]	3.4	3.0	2.4	3.4	5.8	9.7	9.6	9.0

Notes: Between 1973 and 1983 and between 1993 and 2003 export shares were significantly influenced by oil price developments.

a. Figures refer to the EEC(6) in 1963, EC(9) in 1973, EC(10) in 1983, EU(12) in 1993, EU(25) in 2003 and EU(27) in 2008.
b. Figures refer to the Federal Republic of Germany from 1948 through 1983.
c. Beginning with 1998, figures refer to South Africa only and no longer to the Southern African Customs Union.
d. Hong Kong, China; Malaysia; Republic of Korea; Singapore; Separate Customs Territory of Taiwan, Penghu, Kinmen and Matsu (Taipei, Chinese); and Thailand.

Source: Data from WTO (2009), Table I.6.

Table A10. World merchandise trade value by region and selected economy

Exports growth, %				Imports growth, %		
2000–08	*2007*	*2008*		*2000–08*	*2007*	*2008*
			Merchandise			
12	**16**	**15**	**World**	**12**	**15**	**15**
7	11	11	North America	7	6	8
6	12	12	United States	7	5	7
6	8	9	Canada	7	9	7
12	16	10	European Union (27)	12	16	12
18	**18**	**28**	**Africa**	**17**	**24**	**26**
13	20	16	South Africa	16	12	12
18	12	23	Nigeria[a]	22	35	41
13	16	14	Asia	14	15	20
24	**26**	**17**	**China**	**22**	**21**	**18**
6	10	9	Japan	9	7	23

Note: a. WTO Secretariat estimates.

Source: Data from WTO (2009), Table I.3.

Table A11. Value of global inward FDI stock hosted by SSA (US$ millions)

	1982–90	1991–99	2000–04	2005–08
World inward FDI stock	1,059,574.2	2,666,173.0	6,226,322.8	11,930,906.1
SSA inward FDI stock	31,211.4	60,081.8	128,270.6	265,881.8
SSA % in world	2.9	2.3	2.1	2.2
South Africa	10,409.8	17,398.2	43,189.0	99,135.3
Nigeria	5,260.1	16,303.4	27,326.4	58,144.6
Angola	789.8	3,295.4	11,356.5	15,544.8
Sudan	74.4	283.8	3,060.5	12,208.4
Equatorial Guinea	9.7	356.5	2,985.4	9,790.1
Zambia	2,207.9	3,241.7	4,417.0	6,895.6
Congo	502.3	1,026.3	2,150.1	5,915.6
United Rep. of Tanzania	381.2	826.9	3,575.5	5,590.0
Côte d'Ivoire	784.8	1,563.4	3,039.0	5,086.7
Chad	188.9	343.5	1,876.7	4,099.1
Liberia	1,805.5	2,786.1	3,418.8	3,970.8
Cameroon	992.2	1,174.7	2,236.9	3,641.0
Ghana	284.0	815.9	1,781.9	3,577.7
Ethiopia	–	348.5	1,668.7	3,363.9
Namibia	1,959.7	1,676.5	2,177.2	3,141.4
Mozambique	14.6	386.8	1,847.2	3,109.7
Uganda	10.8	282.8	1,182.0	3,070.9
Madagascar	64.5	179.6	195.9	1,579.6
Kenya	517.5	741.2	994.0	1,539.3
Zimbabwe	223.9	605.3	1,259.9	1,460.4
Dem. Rep. of Congo	600.3	561.2	818.3	1,437.5
Guinea	27.7	155.1	335.4	1,204.8
Mauritius	70.8	276.3	709.3	1,148.9
Seychelles	155.6	340.7	618.5	1,091.7
Mali	218.1	289.1	461.2	974.3
Gabon	960.4	815.0	246.1	829.0
Togo	222.0	305.2	535.0	813.4
Senegal	199.3	376.4	303.6	804.5
Swaziland	216.7	469.2	629.9	786.8
Botswana	1,035.9	1,183.5	1,243.7	786.4
Lesotho	37.5	182.6	395.7	708.7
Cape Verde	2.7	50.1	248.4	669.9

Table A11. (continued)

	1982–90	1991–99	2000–04	2005–08
Malawi	182.7	239.7	427.9	564.0
Gambia	132.4	186.1	261.4	479.7
Benin	–	49.0	212.7	475.5
Sierra Leone	261.6	243.0	313.8	393.2
Eritrea	–	162.6	366.3	382.8
Burkina Faso	29.1	63.8	33.6	375.2
Central African Rep.	83.4	86.6	126.4	282.9
Niger	231.5	297.8	74.2	240.3
Somalia	28.8	2.9	3.5	186.4
Rwanda	3.6	50.8	60.0	156.0
São Tomé and Principe	0.4	2.3	18.1	94.5
Guinea-Bissau	3.9	23.5	42.4	82.6
Burundi	25.3	33.1	46.8	47.8
Comoros	7.5	19.4	22.3	30.5

Source: Data from UNCTAD (2009).

Table A12. Shares of global inward FDI stock hosted by SSA

		1982–90	1991–99	2000–04	2005–08	rank
	World (US$ millions)	**1,059,574.2**	**2,666,173.0**	**6,226,322.8**	**11,930,906.1**	
SSA	**SSA (US$ millions)**	**31,211.4**	**60,081.8**	**128,270.6**	**265,881.8**	
rank	**SSA % in world**	**2.9%**	**2.3%**	**2.1%**	**2.2%**	
1	South Africa	0.982%	0.653%	0.694%	0.831%	26
2	Nigeria	0.496%	0.611%	0.439%	0.487%	42
3	Angola	0.075%	0.124%	0.182%	0.130%	65
4	Sudan	0.007%	0.011%	0.049%	0.102%	73
5	Equatorial Guinea	0.001%	0.013%	0.048%	0.082%	82
6	Zambia	0.208%	0.122%	0.071%	0.058%	92
7	Congo	0.047%	0.038%	0.035%	0.050%	95
8	United Rep. of Tanzania	0.036%	0.031%	0.057%	0.047%	96
9	Côte d'Ivoire	0.074%	0.059%	0.049%	0.043%	102
10	Chad	0.018%	0.013%	0.030%	0.034%	106
11	Liberia	0.170%	0.104%	0.055%	0.033%	107
12	Cameroon	0.094%	0.044%	0.036%	0.031%	110
13	Ghana	0.027%	0.031%	0.029%	0.030%	112
14	Ethiopia	–	0.013%	0.027%	0.028%	114
15	Namibia	0.185%	0.063%	0.035%	0.026%	117
16	Mozambique	0.001%	0.015%	0.030%	0.026%	118
17	Uganda	0.001%	0.011%	0.019%	0.026%	120
18	Madagascar	0.006%	0.007%	0.003%	0.013%	136
19	Kenya	0.049%	0.028%	0.016%	0.013%	134
20	Zimbabwe	0.021%	0.023%	0.020%	0.012%	135
21	Dem. Rep. of Congo	0.057%	0.021%	0.013%	0.012%	138
22	Guinea	0.003%	0.006%	0.005%	0.010%	145
23	Mauritius	0.007%	0.010%	0.011%	0.010%	147
24	Seychelles	0.015%	0.013%	0.010%	0.009%	149
25	Mali	0.021%	0.011%	0.007%	0.008%	151
26	Gabon	0.091%	0.031%	0.004%	0.007%	160
27	Togo	0.021%	0.011%	0.009%	0.007%	156
28	Senegal	0.019%	0.014%	0.005%	0.007%	162
29	Swaziland	0.020%	0.018%	0.010%	0.007%	158
30	Botswana	0.098%	0.044%	0.020%	0.007%	159
31	Lesotho	0.004%	0.007%	0.006%	0.006%	165
32	Cape Verde	0.000%	0.002%	0.004%	0.006%	168

Table A12. (continued)

		1982–90	1991–99	2000–04	2005–08	rank
33	Malawi	0.017%	0.009%	0.007%	0.005%	170
34	Gambia	0.012%	0.007%	0.004%	0.004%	173
35	Benin	–	0.002%	0.003%	0.004%	174
36	Sierra Leone	0.025%	0.009%	0.005%	0.003%	177
37	Eritrea	–	0.006%	0.006%	0.003%	178
38	Burkina Faso	0.003%	0.002%	0.001%	0.003%	179
39	Central African Rep.	0.008%	0.003%	0.002%	0.002%	181
40	Niger	0.022%	0.011%	0.001%	0.002%	183
41	Somalia	0.003%	0.000%	0.000%	0.002%	186
42	Rwanda	0.000%	0.002%	0.001%	0.001%	188
43	São Tomé & Principe	0.000%	0.000%	0.000%	0.001%	194
44	Guinea-Bissau	0.000%	0.001%	0.001%	0.001%	195
45	Burundi	0.002%	0.001%	0.001%	0.000%	200
46	Comoros	0.001%	0.001%	0.000%	0.000%	202

Source: Data from UNCTAD (2009).

Table A13. Growth of global inward FDI stock hosted by SSA

		Average percentage change, year-on-year					Average
		1982–90	1991–99	2000–04	2005–08	1982–08	1982–08
	World FDI Stock	11%	11%	15%	12%	12%	**3,282,132.2**
Rank	**SSA inward FDI stock**	20%	23%	16%	28%	21%	**93,445.4**
1	São Tomé & Principe	24%	234%	27%	57%	95%	25.4
2	Guinea-Bissau	197%	20%	5%	23%	77%	29.2
3	Somalia	56%	45%	-2%	195%	63%	46.6
4	Guinea	155%	17%	14%	55%	57%	323.4
5	Equatorial Guinea	78%	58%	43%	22%	56%	2,125.3
6	Mozambique	54%	57%	17%	12%	42%	936.6
7	Uganda	-2%	103%	20%	26%	41%	771.7
8	Cape Verde	11%	59%	17%	33%	37%	190.7
9	Eritrea	–	113%	4%	0%	30%	308.7
10	Sudan	3%	50%	40%	32%	30%	2,494.8
11	Benin	–	19%	44%	27%	29%	197.5
12	Burkina Faso	8%	3%	39%	108%	27%	92.8
13	Ethiopia	–	37%	26%	10%	27%	1,446.3
14	Angola	33%	25%	15%	30%	27%	5,767.7
15	Madagascar	12%	11%	4%	112%	25%	351.7
16	Comoros	49%	2%	3%	15%	20%	17.6
17	Lesotho	27%	16%	10%	18%	19%	251.7
18	Mauritius	23%	10%	16%	22%	17%	417.3
19	Chad	9%	7%	50%	14%	17%	1,132.3
20	Congo	6%	14%	7%	41%	14%	1,784.1
21	Rwanda	–	7%	3%	43%	14%	52.4
22	South Africa	-4%	32%	9%	17%	14%	31,954.0
23	Nigeria	13%	11%	7%	28%	13%	20,862.3
24	United Rep. of Tanzania	1%	24%	20%	9%	13%	1,893.0
25	Ghana	3%	19%	7%	32%	13%	1,226.6
26	Senegal	5%	6%	10%	44%	12%	367.3
27	Seychelles	10%	10%	9%	21%	11%	441.7
28	Mali	1%	2%	41%	10%	10%	398.8
29	Niger	5%	-8%	25%	43%	10%	225.8
30	Côte d'Ivoire	6%	8%	18%	10%	10%	2,099.1
31	Cameroon	11%	4%	16%	8%	9%	1,675.9

Table A13. (continued)

		Average percentage change, year-on-year					Average
		1982–90	1991–99	2000–04	2005–08	1982–08	1982–08
32	Gabon	9%	-18%	–	48%	9%	852.9
33	Zimbabwe	4%	19%	1%	5%	9%	726.1
34	Central African Rep.	6%	1%	10%	26%	8%	122.0
35	Namibia	1%	-2%	39%	0%	7%	2,080.6
36	Kenya	6%	2%	6%	19%	7%	831.7
37	Dem. Rep. of Congo	-3%	1%	11%	34%	6%	751.7
38	Togo	4%	4%	11%	9%	6%	395.3
39	Malawi	5%	5%	12%	3%	6%	303.6
40	Swaziland	6%	6%	16%	-8%	6%	461.9
41	Gambia	2%	4%	9%	16%	6%	225.7
42	Zambia	3%	4%	6%	14%	6%	3,656.1
43	Liberia	11%	2%	3%	3%	5%	2,751.9
44	Burundi	6%	2%	7%	1%	4%	35.2
45	Sierra Leone	-1%	0%	9%	6%	2%	284.5
46	Botswana	6%	1%	-2%	-8%	1%	1,086.6

Source: Data from UNCTAD (2009).

Table A14. Inward FDI flows to SSA as share of world inward FDI flows

Rank SSA		1982–90	1991–99	2000–04	2005–08	World rank out of 233
	World (US$ million)	**109,232.6**	**398,193.1**	**790,978.0**	**1,527,648.6**	
	SSA (US$ million)	1,440.4	5,066.0	13,633.2	44,230.4	
	SSA (%) in world total	**1.3%**	**1.3%**	**1.7%**	**2.9%**	
1	Nigeria	0.563%	0.389%	0.226%	0.846%	24
2	Angola	0.093%	0.170%	0.441%	0.674%	29
3	South Africa	0.001%	0.239%	0.273%	0.341%	47
4	Sudan	0.001%	0.027%	0.115%	0.178%	62
5	Congo	0.023%	0.032%	0.017%	0.112%	76
6	Equatorial Guinea	0.003%	0.028%	0.113%	0.107%	79
7	Ghana	0.007%	0.031%	0.014%	0.061%	94
8	Zambia	0.071%	0.033%	0.031%	0.053%	96
9	Madagascar	0.007%	0.005%	0.011%	0.043%	103
10	Uganda	-0.001%	0.020%	0.026%	0.042%	105
11	United Rep. of Tanzania	0.003%	0.034%	0.045%	0.041%	107
12	Namibia	0.008%	0.024%	0.028%	0.036%	108
13	Chad	0.013%	0.006%	0.068%	0.034%	111
14	Guinea	0.007%	0.005%	0.006%	0.032%	113
15	Dem. Rep. of Congo	-0.024%	0.001%	0.010%	0.025%	121
16	Côte d'Ivoire	0.042%	0.055%	0.030%	0.023%	124
17	Mozambique	0.003%	0.025%	0.033%	0.021%	125
18	Senegal	0.008%	0.014%	0.008%	0.021%	126
19	Botswana	0.053%	0.002%	0.033%	0.021%	127
20	Ethiopia	0.000%	0.021%	0.044%	0.018%	133
21	Cameroon	0.059%	0.011%	0.039%	0.018%	135
22	Kenya	0.027%	0.004%	0.007%	0.015%	137
23	Mauritius	0.014%	0.007%	0.009%	0.014%	139
24	Seychelles	0.012%	0.009%	0.006%	0.014%	140
25	Gabon	0.065%	-0.039%	0.011%	0.013%	142
26	Cape Verde	0.001%	0.004%	0.005%	0.010%	149
27	Burkina Faso	0.002%	0.002%	0.002%	0.009%	152
28	Mali	0.002%	0.007%	0.017%	0.008%	158
29	Benin	0.013%	0.009%	0.006%	0.008%	159
30	Liberia	0.160%	0.014%	0.012%	0.008%	162
31	Lesotho	0.007%	0.006%	0.005%	0.007%	163

Table A14. (continued)

Rank SSA		1982–90	1991–99	2000–04	2005–08	World rank out of 233
32	Niger	0.010%	0.002%	0.002%	0.006%	165
33	Somalia	-0.004%	0.000%	0.000%	0.006%	167
34	Togo	0.008%	0.003%	0.006%	0.004%	169
35	Sierra Leone	-0.009%	0.000%	0.003%	0.004%	170
36	Zimbabwe	0.009%	0.026%	0.002%	0.004%	171
37	Gambia	0.003%	0.005%	0.005%	0.004%	172
38	Central African Rep.	0.004%	0.000%	0.002%	0.004%	173
39	Rwanda	0.014%	0.001%	0.001%	0.003%	174
40	Malawi	0.008%	0.003%	0.007%	0.002%	177
41	São Tomé & Principe	0.000%	0.000%	0.000%	0.002%	181
42	Guinea-Bissau	0.001%	0.001%	0.000%	0.001%	186
43	Swaziland	0.025%	0.017%	0.006%	0.001%	189
44	Comoros	0.003%	0.000%	0.000%	0.000%	192
45	Burundi	0.001%	0.000%	0.000%	0.000%	202
46	Eritrea	0.000%	0.019%	0.002%	0.000%	230

Source: Data from UNCTAD (2009).

Table A15. SSA inward FDI stock as percentage of GDP PPP

		2002	2003	2004	2005	2006	2007	2008	2002–08
	All SSA GDP (US$ Billions)	1,094.1	1,155.2	1,211.6	1,331.3	1,480.1	1,710.6	1,596.2	1,368.4
	All SSA FDI/GDP	10%	12%	14%	15%	16%	17%	22%	15%
	Mean shares	20.7%	22.6%	26.9%	29.4%	21.2%	22.0%	25.9%	24.1%
1	Equatorial Guinea	229.0%	278.5%	388.7%	508.9%	33.3%	38.8%	49.5%	218.1%
2	Liberia	90.1%	99.5%	109.3%	120.9%	142.3%	140.0%	261.1%	137.6%
3	Seychelles	112.3%	109.1%	114.6%	127.7%	142.4%	179.1%	100.1%	126.5%
4	Congo	78.5%	90.7%	114.3%	119.8%	186.4%	124.9%	65.9%	111.5%
5	Zambia	50.1%	51.1%	60.4%	53.4%	58.2%	66.3%	53.2%	56.1%
6	Angola	94.1%	69.6%	64.4%	51.6%	31.2%	20.3%	33.6%	52.1%
7	Cape Verde	39.6%	47.9%	56.1%	61.6%	20.7%	31.7%	32.8%	41.5%
8	Nigeria	24.8%	25.0%	28.6%	28.3%	38.2%	31.0%	28.0%	29.1%
9	São Tomé & Principe	8.8%	10.2%	11.4%	18.1%	33.7%	47.4%	60.9%	27.2%
10	Chad	21.1%	26.3%	27.4%	19.3%	20.6%	29.8%	33.2%	25.4%
11	Namibia	22.2%	22.2%	29.7%	16.6%	16.6%	25.0%	32.5%	23.5%
12	United Rep. of Tanzania	14.3%	18.3%	21.7%	17.1%	20.4%	18.9%	15.4%	18.0%
13	Gambia	10.2%	10.3%	12.5%	13.0%	15.0%	15.4%	43.1%	17.1%
14	Côte d'Ivoire	10.8%	14.0%	17.2%	15.0%	17.7%	19.8%	18.7%	16.2%
15	South Africa	7.5%	11.0%	14.1%	16.0%	16.4%	18.9%	25.6%	15.6%
16	Swaziland	12.9%	14.1%	16.2%	13.6%	13.2%	14.8%	11.4%	13.7%
17	Mozambique	10.5%	12.5%	10.8%	11.3%	10.9%	10.3%	20.2%	12.4%
18	Lesotho	7.1%	8.5%	8.6%	9.0%	10.4%	12.8%	29.3%	12.2%
19	Sudan	5.3%	7.1%	7.2%	10.1%	13.0%	14.5%	16.5%	10.5%
20	Eritrea	11.2%	12.1%	12.3%	9.3%	8.0%	7.8%	7.8%	9.8%
21	Cameroon	8.3%	9.9%	10.3%	10.3%	10.7%	8.4%	9.8%	9.7%
22	Sierra Leone	10.8%	9.4%	12.7%	8.4%	8.4%	7.1%	8.6%	9.4%
23	Togo	6.9%	7.1%	7.6%	7.9%	8.4%	8.7%	17.7%	9.2%
24	Zimbabwe	4.5%	4.2%	5.3%	5.7%	5.5%	5.8%	25.1%	8.0%
25	Mali	5.5%	6.8%	7.0%	7.9%	8.2%	6.2%	7.6%	7.0%
26	Ghana	4.4%	4.3%	4.4%	4.4%	5.2%	5.9%	17.9%	6.6%
27	Malawi	5.5%	5.3%	7.9%	6.9%	6.9%	7.2%	5.8%	6.5%
28	Mauritius	5.3%	5.6%	5.5%	5.1%	5.6%	7.3%	11.0%	6.5%
29	Comoros	5.1%	5.1%	5.2%	5.2%	6.0%	7.6%	9.5%	6.2%
30	Guinea-Bissau	3.5%	4.2%	3.8%	5.7%	6.4%	7.0%	12.2%	6.1%
31	Guinea	1.9%	2.1%	2.4%	2.9%	3.3%	5.2%	24.5%	6.1%

Table A15. (continued)

		2002	2003	2004	2005	2006	2007	2008	2002–08
32	Uganda	3.9%	4.2%	4.4%	4.9%	5.6%	5.9%	12.6%	5.9%
33	Madagascar	1.3%	2.0%	1.8%	1.7%	5.6%	10.5%	17.0%	5.7%
34	Botswana	6.9%	7.8%	7.1%	5.3%	4.9%	4.2%	2.6%	5.6%
35	Central African Rep.	2.4%	2.9%	3.7%	4.7%	4.9%	5.5%	13.4%	5.4%
36	Ethiopia	3.3%	4.0%	5.4%	4.8%	5.6%	4.7%	6.9%	5.0%
37	Gabon	0.0%	0.0%	3.3%	6.0%	9.2%	9.9%	5.2%	4.8%
38	Benin	2.5%	3.1%	3.4%	3.2%	4.4%	6.3%	5.6%	4.1%
39	Dem. Rep. of Congo	2.5%	2.8%	2.8%	2.2%	1.6%	3.3%	12.8%	4.0%
40	Kenya	3.1%	3.2%	3.4%	3.0%	2.8%	4.3%	3.4%	3.3%
41	Senegal	1.4%	2.2%	2.5%	1.9%	2.3%	3.7%	7.3%	3.1%
42	Somalia	0.1%	0.1%	0.0%	0.4%	2.2%	4.7%	6.3%	2.0%
43	Niger	0.8%	0.9%	1.3%	1.0%	1.6%	2.1%	4.7%	1.8%
44	Burkina Faso	0.2%	0.4%	0.3%	0.5%	1.0%	2.8%	4.1%	1.3%
45	Rwanda	0.8%	0.7%	0.7%	0.7%	0.9%	1.1%	2.8%	1.1%
46	Burundi	1.2%	1.3%	1.3%	1.2%	1.0%	0.8%	0.7%	1.1%

Source: Data from UNCTAD (2009).

Table A16. Inward FDI flows to SSA as percentage of GDP PPP

		2002	2003	2004	2005	2006	2007	2008	2002–08
	All SSA GDP (US$ billions)	**1,094.1**	**1,155.2**	**1,211.6**	**1,331.3**	**1,480.1**	**1,710.6**	**1,596.2**	**1,368.4**
	All SSA FDI/GDP %	**1.2%**	**1.5%**	**1.4%**	**2.1%**	**2.5%**	**2.7%**	**4.1%**	**2.2%**
1	Equatorial Guinea	30.9%	104.7%	116.9%	129.5%	6.1%	6.2%	5.3%	57.1%
2	Angola	22.2%	33.0%	26.9%	28.9%	23.4%	17.8%	19.5%	24.5%
3	Congo	4.9%	12.1%	-0.6%	21.1%	74.1%	34.1%	18.6%	23.5%
4	Seychelles	7.8%	9.3%	6.0%	13.6%	22.9%	37.2%	24.2%	17.3%
5	Cape Verde	6.3%	5.8%	11.7%	13.9%	5.0%	7.5%	7.0%	8.2%
6	São Tomé & Principe	1.8%	1.6%	1.6%	7.0%	16.2%	14.7%	13.6%	8.1%
7	Zambia	3.5%	3.8%	4.3%	3.5%	5.9%	11.5%	5.8%	5.5%
8	Chad	10.0%	7.0%	4.1%	-0.6%	3.7%	4.8%	5.3%	4.9%
9	Nigeria	1.9%	1.9%	1.9%	3.9%	10.6%	6.1%	6.8%	4.7%
10	Liberia	0.1%	10.2%	2.2%	2.6%	3.9%	4.6%	9.0%	4.7%
11	Namibia	2.2%	1.1%	1.6%	2.3%	2.3%	4.8%	7.0%	3.1%
12	Sudan	1.4%	2.5%	2.0%	3.0%	4.1%	2.6%	2.6%	2.6%
13	Guinea	0.2%	0.5%	0.5%	0.5%	0.6%	1.8%	13.6%	2.5%
14	Gabon	0.5%	2.7%	4.3%	3.0%	3.2%	2.6%	0.1%	2.4%
15	Madagascar	0.4%	0.7%	0.7%	0.6%	1.8%	4.4%	7.6%	2.3%
16	Botswana	3.3%	2.8%	2.8%	1.8%	3.0%	2.5%	0.0%	2.3%
17	Gambia	1.7%	0.6%	1.9%	1.6%	2.4%	2.3%	4.6%	2.1%
18	Lesotho	0.5%	0.8%	1.0%	1.0%	1.5%	1.8%	6.2%	1.8%
19	United Rep. of Tanzania	1.7%	1.4%	1.5%	1.9%	2.3%	2.1%	1.7%	1.8%
20	Mozambique	2.0%	1.9%	1.1%	0.5%	0.6%	1.4%	3.1%	1.5%
21	Ghana	0.1%	0.2%	0.3%	0.3%	1.2%	1.4%	6.6%	1.5%
22	Mali	2.6%	1.3%	0.9%	2.0%	0.7%	0.5%	0.9%	1.3%
23	Sierra Leone	0.4%	0.3%	2.1%	2.3%	1.1%	1.7%	0.6%	1.2%
24	Uganda	0.6%	0.6%	0.8%	0.9%	1.3%	1.3%	2.4%	1.1%
25	Central African Rep.	0.1%	0.5%	0.6%	0.8%	0.7%	1.1%	4.0%	1.1%
26	Cameroon	2.2%	1.4%	1.1%	0.7%	0.9%	0.6%	0.6%	1.1%
27	Côte d'Ivoire	0.8%	0.7%	1.2%	1.2%	1.2%	1.5%	1.1%	1.1%
28	Senegal	0.5%	0.3%	0.4%	0.2%	1.1%	1.3%	3.3%	1.0%
29	Dem. Rep. of Congo	0.4%	0.5%	0.0%	-0.2%	-0.2%	1.6%	5.1%	1.0%
30	Benin	0.2%	0.6%	0.8%	0.6%	0.6%	2.9%	1.0%	1.0%
31	Somalia	0.0%	0.0%	-0.1%	0.5%	1.8%	2.6%	1.6%	0.9%
32	Guinea-Bissau	0.3%	0.4%	0.1%	0.9%	1.5%	1.4%	1.7%	0.9%